# Date Due

| | | |
|---|---|---|
| MAY 31 1986 | | |
| MAY 28 1987 | | |
| DEC 21 1993 | APR 24 2006 | |
| OCT 26 1994 | | |
| SEP 25 1998 | APR 14 2008 | APR 14 2008 |
| FEB 23 2001 | | |
| | APR 30 2008 | |
| AUG 07 2003 | MAY 14 2008 | |
| | | |
| | | |
| | | |
| | | |

# DISASTERS THAT MADE HISTORY

# DISASTERS THAT MADE HISTORY
## Webb Garrison

ABINGDON PRESS ● Nashville and New York

DISASTERS THAT MADE HISTORY

*Library of Congress Cataloging in Publication Data*

GARRISON, WEBB B. Disasters that made history.
Bibliography: p.      1. Disasters—United States.
I. Title.
E179.G25        973        72-6995

ISBN  0-687-10795-4

MANUFACTURED BY THE PARTHENON PRESS, AT
NASHVILLE, TENNESSEE, UNITED STATES OF AMERICA

For
*Henry and Mae*

# Preface

Whether natural or triggered by man, catastrophic events are giant-size slices from the stuff of everyday life. Heroism, greed, courage, and cowardice are magnified by the events in which they are interwoven.

Small wonder, therefore, that disasters are high on the list of human-interest events that constitute the raw material of history. Unfortunately most readily available works do little more than give dates, casualties, and causes of sudden death and destruction in the past, or deal with events around a single category or which depict traumatic moments in history.

The present volume has a different focus.

While it obviously is impossible to treat catastrophic events without depicting some of violence inherent in them, the variety of individual disasters here described have more than local or momentary significance. Some of them show how quickly "civilized" persons can descend to the level of animals clawing for a chance to live. Others depict the finest and best in human nature.

Many case histories included in this volume led to changes or triggered reforms or initiated new ways of dealing with age-old problems. Hence this compilation is one index to the human condition. Ceaselessly prone to titanic assaults from nature and vulnerable to his own weaknesses, it is basic to man's nature that the typical response to overwhelming catastrophe is to start over and try to do things better.

Social and individual failures that led to some of the events here described usually—not always, but usually!—spurred stronger efforts or inspired new ideas. As a result the long-range effects of events involving carelessness or bad judgment or haste or greed or those uncontrollable eruptions that by a quirk of speech we insist upon calling "acts of God" have saved more lives than they have claimed.

Long-range effects cannot be assessed at once. For this reason, only those disasters that can be viewed from a distance of about a quarter of a century are described. It will be instantly apparent that those most widely known and about which information is readily available—the San Francisco earthquake, the Chicago fire, the sinking of the *Titanic*, and the like—have been bypassed.

My wife, Mary, was intimately involved in the entire process of selection of topics, research, and production of finished manuscript. My son, Bill, spent day after day with photocopy machines and microfilm print-out machines. Vignettes presented here have been distilled from more than 7,500 pages of raw material.

Some of these graphic moments are based on briefer articles written by me for a variety of periodicals. I should like to express appreciation to the editors and readers of *Coronet, Pageant, Blue Book, Saga, Catholic Digest,* and *Your Life* magazines.

Special gratitude is due publisher Generoso Pope, Jr., of the *National Enquirer.* Along with articles editor Joseph Cassidy, Mr. Pope led me to a new understanding of the way disasters often have positive long-range effects as a result of reforms initiated in their wake.

Disaster articles published in the media listed above have brought me into personal contact with survivors, or descendants of survivors, of nearly every catastrophe described.

Though the stories told have already gone into history books, they are strangely contemporary. Most communities presently have sets of conditions conducive to repetition of at least one cataclysmic event described in these pages.

Webb Garrison

# Contents

*Middle western and eastern United States
December 16, 1811, to February 7, 1812*

# 1 The Earthquake of 1811

"On the 16th of December, 1811, about two o'clock in the morning, we were awakened by violent trembling of the earth. It was accompanied by a very awful noise that resembled loud but distant thunder. The whole atmosphere was quickly saturated with sulphurous vapor.

"The screams of inhabitants, the cries of fowls and beasts of every species, the falling trees, and the roaring of the Mississippi —whose current was retrograde for a few minutes—formed a scene of horror beyond power of words to convey."

Writing to her pastor, Methodist circuit rider Lorenzo Dow, Eliza Bryan of New Madrid, Missouri, gave one of the most objective eyewitness accounts of the worst recorded United States earthquake.

Members of several Indian tribes that lived and hunted in the Mississippi Valley had told early white explorers that the Great Spirit sometimes stamped his feet and made the earth tremble.

White men brushed off these tales as a product of the Indians' superstition. Europeans, notably in Italy, had experienced

11

enough earthquakes to begin to have a glimmer of understanding about their scope and power. Most men of learning agreed that the North American continent was too vast and too strong ever to be troubled by quaking of the earth.

These naïve views were quashed by quakes plus secondary tremors that continued over a period of nearly two months after the initial shock described by Eliza Bryan.

Area shaken amounted to at least one million square miles. Chimneys were demolished in St. Louis, Cincinnati, and Louisville. Bricks fell in Georgia and South Carolina.

Tremors were felt at New Orleans, 500 miles away; at Detroit, 600 miles away; and even at Boston, 1100 miles away. In the nation's capital, 700 miles from the epicenter of the quake, the vibrations were strong enough to cause a general alarm.

On three separate occasions—December 16, 1811; January 23, and February 7, 1812—magnitude of tremors reached 10, the top of the earthquake scale. More than 2600 separate sets of vibrations were recorded at Louisville, Kentucky.

Topographic changes were on so vast a scale that they are just now being accurately measured by means of aerial photography. But because the section hardest hit was sparsely settled and had no buildings except quake resistant log cabins, only one fatality was reported.

"Had the New Madrid earthquake occurred 150 years later," according to experts of the U. S. Geological Survey, "tens of thousands of persons would have died and property damage would have been many times that suffered in the San Francisco earthquake and fire."

Eyewitness accounts, often exaggerated as a result of near-hysteria, sound like Old Testament descriptions of the mighty deeds of an angry Jehovah.

"A small river called the Pemiseo, probably a tributary of the St. Francis, then ran a southwest course," according to James Ritchie, who packed what belongings he could salvage and hurried to Illinois after the quake.

"For a distance of nearly fifty miles the Pemiseo blew up. Its bed was entirely destroyed. The earth would open in fissures from forty to eighty rods in length and from three to five feet in width. Their depth none knew, as no one had strength of nerve sufficient to fathom them."

Large forest trees which stood in the track of fissures actually did split from root to branch. Courses of streams changed. Bottoms of lakes were pushed upward as much as fifteen feet. Dry land blew up, settled down, and formed lakes of dark, muddy water.

Reelfoot Lake in northwestern Tennessee was the most spectacular permanent formation. Today the shallow lake is about eighteen miles long, five miles wide. Pioneers actually caught in the most severely shaken region did not know that the lake suddenly came into existence as a result of a sharp drop in level of land.

Descriptions probably can't be taken literally, but there is every reason to believe that both the mighty Mississippi and the Ohio actually flowed backward for a brief interval in the aftermath of the December shock.

Lore of many peoples, including the followers of Moses, includes accounts of the earth moving in waves and the sudden production of huge fissures. Such tales had been regarded as pure fiction. Now the region about New Madrid was split and pockmarked in such fashion that no observer could deny what had happened.

Many immense holes and fissures gradually filled with sand. Consequently they are still easily discovered from the air.

In the aftermath of the quake the United States government launched its first program of disaster relief. So many farms were ruined in regions of the hardest shocks that any owner who could prove his loss was offered, gratis, an entire section of 640 acres in the Boon Lick region of western Kentucky.

Political and military consequences were far greater than might be thought since the hardest-hit area of 30,000 to 50,000 square miles had only scattered settlements of whites.

Tecumseh, noted chief of the Shawnees, had already taken the lead in trying to unite western Indians against the white man. His brother, a powerful medicine man, had promised to persuade the Great Spirit to stamp his foot and frighten white men away from the frontier.

Tribesmen led by Tecumseh were crushed by whites under

13

the command of William Henry Harrison, at the Battle of Tippecanoe in November, 1811. Weeks later, during one of many tribal ceremonies led by Shawnee medicine men, North America experienced the most violent earthquake on record. It was noted and reported by Indian tribes as far away as Canada.

Made bold by this sign of support, the tribes allied under the leadership of Tecumseh made fresh efforts to stem the westward flow of settlers—and as a result were banished to reservations in faraway Oklahoma.

Effects upon systematic study of earthquakes, then in its infancy, were immediate and long-reaching. For the first time U. S. geologists took seriously the fact that the great North American continent becomes highly vulnerable under the right combination of forces and circumstances.

Initially at New Harmony, Indiana, and later at the nation's capital, scientists began to accumulate data and to study theories about the causes of earthquakes. One of the world's great centers for study of geology, a department of St. Louis University, came into existence partly because the quakes of 1811-12 showed the midsection of the continent to be highly vulnerable.

An elaborate study by the U. S. Geological Survey, timed for release one hundred years after the New Madrid quake, reported the disaster as "unquestionably due to a fracture in deep-seated rocks, probably a further adjustment of an old break."

It could happen again, geologists warn.

Californians who fear that part of the state will break off and drop into the Pacific are prone to look with longing at the "safe and secure Midwest." Some groups have actually emigrated to Indiana and Tennessee in search of an earthquake-free haven.

"If it showed nothing else, the great series of quakes in 1811-12 showed that no place is safe," naturalist John James Audubon confided to his diary.

"When one of the shocks came, I was exploring in Kentucky. I thought my horse had suddenly foundered; he seemed about to die. At that instant all the shrubs and trees began to move from their very roots. The ground rose in successive furrows, like the ruffled waters of a lake, and I became bewildered in all my senses."

Audubon's verdict is right, say present-day experts. There is

14

no absolutely safe place. But studies triggered by America's most devastating response to the stamping of the Great Spirit's foot have affected building practices so greatly that danger of disastrous effects from quakes has been considerably reduced.

Reelfoot Lake is now one of the fastest-growing United States tourist attractions!

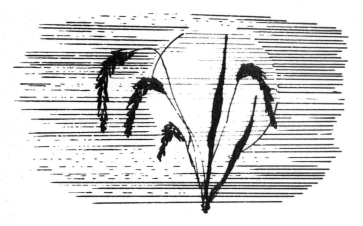

*Summer, 1816*
*New England*

# 2 Year Without a Summer

Weatherwise, 1816 started off in normal fashion. New Englanders consulted their almanacs and began calculating weeks ahead to the time of spring plowing and planting.

As usual April brought noticeably warmer days. Migratory birds began to return to their old haunts. Buds swelled and then began to burst in nature's silent signal: "Spring is here!"

May was not significantly warmer than April, though. Sparse records of the era indicate that in some regions the month was actually colder than April. Dawn after dawn householders rose early with the hope of finding the ground clear, but instead were greeted by heavy frost.

A few villagers who relied chiefly on the calendar instead of the thermometer put out household fires for the year. Most of their neighbors kept fires smoldering, for the nights were still uncomfortable—even to hardy folk who slept on feather beds and covered themselves with many layers of quilts.

"Be patient," was the typical attitude. "Good Old Mother

Nature is just a bit sluggish this year. When she wakes up, summer will come with a bang."

June 6 quashed all such notions.

That day ten inches of snow fell across much of New England. Connecticut was caught in a blinding blizzard. Where strong winds blew, snowdrifts were more than two feet deep.

Instead of proving to be winter's last fling that June snowstorm was simply a prelude to a summer that has no equal in recorded history. Modern meteorologists often label 1816 as "the Year Without a Summer." New Englanders, whose tongues were still colored with the flavor of picturesque Elizabethan speech, bluntly termed it "eighteen hundred and froze to death."

Ground thawed briefly at intervals—then froze harder than before. Except for a few hours at a time on sunny afternoons, thermometers stayed in the 30's.

A few optimistic farmers who planted "by the almanac" had managed to get seeds in the ground approximately on schedule. Those plants that sprouted were killed by heavy frosts and by freezing nights.

Matters improved a trifle in July and August. Many days the temperature at sunrise was in the low 40's. But September brought another downward dip. Half an inch of ice formed a miniature glacier that gradually spread over most of Vermont and New Hampshire.

Farmers were in trouble as far away as northern Indiana and Illinois, where crops were planted as many as four or five times —always to be stunted or killed by new blasts of icy wind. Crops were ravaged by frost, snow, sleet, and hail in areas that now make up about forty states.

On July 4, Savannah, Georgia, registered a high temperature of 46°.

Three thousand miles to the east, England, Ireland, Scotland, and Wales were hit hard, too. Many farmers succeeded in bringing some crops to maturity, but grain was light in weight and potatoes were scrawny. France and Germany were seriously affected. Even Spain and Italy did not escape without damage to crops.

Descendants of Puritans pulled down their Old Testaments

17

and thoughtfully thumbed through them, pondering passages about "the wrath of a vengeful God." Many ministers, notably in and about the Boston area, preached sermon after sermon warning their listeners that the end of time was at hand.

"Sin has brought on this change in the course of Nature," declared the Rev. Franklin Palmer of Boston. "The skies themselves are pleading with this infant nation, 'Turn from your wicked ways!' "

Weather scientists were scarce, and most were self-taught. No U.S. institution offered comprehensive training in the analysis of weather, and "forecasting" consisted almost entirely of projecting one year's weather from records of previous years.

Some skeptics muttered their doubts that the end of time was at hand, but few made public statements questioning the possibility that the unheard-of weather actually constituted divine punishment for national sin.

It was not until October of 1816 that anyone with a reputation for knowledge of the earth and its mantle of gas that we call the atmosphere put forth a nontheological explanation for that summer which never came.

Prussian astronomer Friedrich W. Bessel, who later gained fame for preparing an amazingly accurate catalog of 3,222 stars on the basis of observations by James Bradley, reported that he had seen "great clouds of dust in the upper atmosphere." This dust, Bessel theorized, might have shielded part of the Northern Hemisphere from the rays of the sun at critical periods.

Investigation not only showed this conjecture to be right; the precise cause of this most fearful case of atmospheric pollution was pinpointed.

Few persons, then or now, could identify the island of Sumbawa in the Dutch East Indies. With an area of about 4300 square miles the island supported a population estimated at no more than 15,000 at its peak. Much of the land could not be cultivated, though the volcano whose cone formed Mt. Tambora was thought to be extinct or "dead."

Sir Stamford Raffles, lieutenant governor of Java, reported that there were minor eruptions of ash and steam late in 1814. The first full-scale detonation, on April 5, 1815, was heard in Sumatra at a distance of 931 miles and taken for artillery.

18

Explosions, mounting in fury, continued for a period of 34 days. So much dust was spewed out that Java, 310 miles away, remained in complete darkness for 4 days. Only 36 natives of Sumbawa escaped.

Tambora's top, reduced to rubble, exploded into the atmosphere. In a circle several miles in diameter, stones as large as a man's head cascaded down. Meanwhile an estimated 100 cubic miles of fine dust spurted into the upper atmosphere.

Added to dust already put there by earlier volcanic eruptions, billions of billions of particles served as a screen separating portions of the planet from the warming rays of our celestial furnace.

All the factories and automobiles and utility plants and schools and private homes in the world do not emit 100 cubic miles of solid matter in a year of operation. Neither do typical activities of man the polluter send particulate matter into the upper atmosphere. Some atomic tests do so, but on a scale that is puny compared with the sudden disintegration of the upper one-third of Mt. Tambora.

It took years of tests and verification to convince skeptics. But within a generation after "eighteen hundred and froze to death" most informed persons were aware that a volcanic eruption in the remote Dutch East Indies actually had brought devastating cold to New England.

Tambora's eruption established, once and for all, the global nature of weather. Tentative and fumbling attempts toward a planetary system of keeping records were launched. For the first time men knew positively that, weatherwise, "no man is an island."

Matters didn't end there, however.

U.S. debate over sponsorship of a fleet of supersonic transports, to operate in the stratosphere at two and one half times the speed of sound, caused environmentalists to rally. Flying at 65,000 feet for a number of years, said opponents, such craft would discharge enough water vapor and particulate matter to have a material effect upon global weather.

In support of that argument, events of 1815-16 in the Dutch East Indies and in New England were described in detail. Many

19

U.S. Congressmen and Senators who had never heard of Mt. Tamboro suddenly became intensely interested in it.

Since economic as well as ecological factors were involved in defeat of the SST program that was backed by the president of the United States plus military leaders and heads of civilian aircraft building firms, it is impossible to precisely pinpoint the effect of Tamboro's eruption on fate of the bill. But future analysts, looking back upon the 1970's, may find that even more than the flow of lava that buried Pompeii, the eruption of Tamboro was a disaster that made history.

*December 16-17, 1835*
*New York City*

# 3  The Fire That Leveled Manhattan

By the 1830's it seemed that the youthful United States had found the path to a never-ending economic boom. Population had soared to more than 12,000,000. The national debt had been retired and the federal government actually had to distribute a surplus among the states.

Manhattan had already begun to emerge as the financial and economic hub of the nation. Prosperous merchants sold their old homes in the heart of the district and moved uptown to the suburbs—beyond 14th Street.

Wall Street, synonymous with big money, was the heart of a booming city of about 250,000. Skylines of that city were still dominated, it is true, with church steeples and chimneys of factories. But financial institutions plus import and export houses concentrated within a few acres controlled much of the wealth of the nation.

Like all other cities of the era New York depended upon volunteers to man the fire department. Political struggles involving the already powerful Tammany Hall organization often affected policy decisions.

Plans had been made to build a series of dams and aqueducts in order to supply Manhattan with water from the Croton River, fifty miles to the north. Such a water supply, some civic leaders urged, could well prove decisive if the city were ever threatened by a serious fire.

Procrastination plus graft plus outright indifference at Tammany Hall stalled the project. Other things—tangible things that persuaded newly arrived immigrants to back the political organization—were more important.

Volunteer fire fighters of Manhattan, headed by Chief Engineer James "Handsome Jim" Gulick, sensed the possibility of trouble during the second week of December, 1835. Snow already packed the streets, and the skies looked as though they held plenty more. Low temperatures caused householders and businessmen alike to keep their fireplaces and potbellied stoves going day and night. A rash of minor fires had brought men of three companies to the point of exhaustion.

Instead of getting better the weather took a turn for the worse. For a period of eight days, temperatures reached sub-zero readings. So much new snow fell that in the financial district it was packed two feet deep.

Most of the city's forty-nine fire engines had made several runs. So had all of the five hose carts and six hook-and-ladder trucks.

At dusk on December 16, a strong north-northwestern wind began to pick up speed and strength. The temperature dropped to $-17°$ and everyone who could do so got off the streets.

That's why no one noticed the first smoke from a splendid five-story building at 25 Merchant Street. By the time the fire was discovered at nine o'clock by insurance watchman Peter Holmes, it was out of control. Flames were already glowing through the windows of three floors.

Holmes relayed an alarm to City Hall, where the great bell was quickly put into action. Bell ringers of fire-alarm stations took up the signal, and soon it was sounding from belfries of the city's churches.

Intense cold hampered operations from the start. Hydrants

yielded so little water that hoses could throw streams only about twenty feet. Anytime an engine stopped working for five minutes, water inside it froze solid.

Chief Gulick ordered several of his companies to the East River. Firemen chopped holes in the ice, then hooked several engines in sequence to form a line long enough to reach flames.

Fire moved far faster than fire fighters. Within an hour after the first alarm at least thirty big buildings were burning.

Both the *Evening Post* and the *Mercantile Advertiser* published hour-by-hour accounts in the aftermath of the holocaust. Brief excerpts from those accounts give some indication of the factors that contributed to disaster:

11:00 P.M. Flames have already reached Water Street. Stores on Exchange Place have taken fire. There simply is not enough water to stop the advance of the flames.

12:00 Midnight. There is little hope of saving any buildings in the Exchange. The Post Office is burning, but firemen hope to save it.

1:00 A.M. Couriers have removed letters and parcels from the doomed Post Office. All Wall Street below William Street appears doomed.

2:00 A.M. Help has arrived. Units have come from Brooklyn, Jersey City, Newark, Hoboken, and Morristown and have reported to Chief Gulick. It is feared that they have come too late.

3:00 A.M. Most of the Exchange is in ruins. Garden Street Church is reported to be on fire, with an unknown person using the organ to play a death march.

Looting is rapidly getting completely out of hand. Reports charge that many volunteer firemen have deserted their engines in order to pillage. One man, discovered applying a torch to a building at Broad Street and Stone, was strung to the nearest tree by self-appointed vigilantes.

4:00 A.M. We have just heard that Mayor Cornelius Lawrence, who was prompt on the scene, has conferred with Chief Gulick about a means to stop the conflagration. Plans are believed to be under way to arrest the flames before they reach Broad Street by blowing up a number of buildings with gunpowder.

5:00 A.M. In obedience to orders from the mayor, a barge dispatched from Governor's Island arrived with a cargo of powder. Sailors under command of Captain Mix have within the hour levelled several buildings along Exchange Place.

23

Wrapped in pea jackets, these brave men transported kegs and barrels of gunpowder amid a constant shower of fire, as they followed their officers to the various buildings designated for destruction.

5:00 A.M. We go to press while the fire is still raging. The exhaustion of the firemen from fatigue and cold is such that we venture to call upon the Citizens to repair to the scene of the conflagration to man the engines and relieve one another.

Heavy wind hampered northerly progress of the fire and checked it in that direction. Foreman Zophar Mills and the men of Engine #13 took their stand on Wall Street at its narrowest point, near the intersections with Water Street and Pearl Street.

Many men poured brandy into their boots to prevent their feet from freezing as they fought the fire.

Several buildings were saved by use of vinegar.

H. R. Downing, famous throughout Manhattan as the "oyster king," then operated a famous restaurant on Broad Street. When firemen could no longer get even a trickle of water, the restaurant-owner donated dozens of barrels of vinegar. Poured into fire engines and pumped from them, the liquid preserved the restaurant plus the *Journal of Commerce* building and smaller structures on both sides.

Shortly after dawn the Franklin Engine Co. of Philadelphia, with a crew of 400 volunteers, reached the stricken city.

Philadelphia firemen had arranged for a special train when news of the magnitude of the blaze reached them. But one section of track was undergoing repair, so the fire engines had to be pulled by manpower across four miles of Jersey marshland frozen by the intense cold.

These men arrived too late to be of much help; by dynamiting buildings in the path of the flames, the fire was contained about 5:15.

The heart of America's financial center lay in ruins. According to a report by the *Courier and Enquirer,* 654 buildings were a total loss. Many others were so badly damaged that they were eventually razed.

Money damage was estimated at about $22,000,000—a stupendous sum for the era. Total fire insurance in force did not exceed half that amount. Most insurance companies went bankrupt, and few claims were ever paid.

Mayor Lawrence was a defendant, along with the city of New York, in many lawsuits that stemmed from the blowing up of buildings. Though no damages were ever assessed, the mayor was harassed for years by appearances in at least thirty-three court actions.

Long-range economic effects were beyond measurement.

Most buildings destroyed by the fire were soon replaced by new and bigger ones built with borrowed money, for the nation was riding a wave of prosperity. Many who rebuilt after securing long-term loans on easy terms found themselves in trouble when the economy began to falter. So many defaulted that most economists list "recovery loans after the Great New York Fire" as precipitating factors helping to plunge the nation into the Panic of 1837. Other effects were more constructive.

Throughout the nation, mayors and fire chiefs demanded money for more and better equipment. Manhattan pushed ahead with the long-deferred Croton water project. When it was completed, a big reservoir at 5th Avenue and 42nd Street assured the city of adequate water to fight future fires.

Other cities piped in water from a distance and built their own reservoirs. The nation's fire hydrants quadrupled in number. The Philadelphia-type fire engine, far more powerful than most others then manufactured, became official equipment in the majority of U. S. urban centers.

Not nearly so familiar as the Chicago fire the great New York fire had far more impact upon the life of the nation. Put to its first decisive test the volunteer system had proved ineffective, not because firemen were cowardly or inefficient, but because New York's department was too deeply involved in politics. Neither men nor equipment were ready to face so decisive a test as that given on the night of December 16 and the morning of December 17.

It would be decades before big cities turned to professional fire fighters in lieu of volunteers. But every municipal system in America was jolted into recognition that Chief Gulick had been right when he warned, months before the holocaust, "You can't play politics with fire."

April 27, 1865
*Mississippi River, near Memphis*

# 4 Explosion of the *Sultana*

No one knows positively how many died when the side-wheel steamer *Sultana* blew up and sank in the early hours of April 27, 1865.

Some trained observers estimated the death toll at about 1,900—probably too high. A U. S. Army board of review tried to minimize the tragedy by publishing a figure of 1,238 dead. All who were personally involved agreed that figure to be absurdly low.

Customs Service officials at Memphis gave out a figure of 1,547. Many standard lists of major disasters rely on that estimate. Even if it is right—which it probably isn't—the *Sultana* took more persons to sudden death than did the universally known *Titanic*.

Most river buffs and Civil War enthusiasts know the general story of the *Sultana*, but among Americans in general the name of the ill-fated vessel evokes no memory. Part of the reason for this historical vacuum is that the tragedy took place during the most tumultuous single month of the nineteenth century.

No one in his right mind would have believed that a proud Mississippi steamer, never more than a few hundred yards from shore, could have caused such carnage.

But from the perspective of more than one hundred years it seems unbelievable that responsible officials could have done what they did.

Vicksburg, Mississippi, was the point of departure for Union soldiers who had been held as prisoners of war at Confederate camps such as Cahaba and Andersonville. Joyful over their freedom, elated at the prospect of returning home, these half-starved scarecrows had faced death so many times that they had lost all fear—and common sense.

Freed prisoners clamored to be put on the very first boat. So they were loaded on upriver steamers in contingents of about one thousand men per vessel.

Late in April, 1865, ugly rumors began spreading.

Officials responsible for arranging passage were said to "have made an arrangement." In return for a kickback of one dollar per head, they were alleged to be putting all ex-prisoners on vessels belonging to a single steamship line.

Arrival of the *Sultana* at Vicksburg, Mississippi, provided a fine chance to scotch this rumor. Built two years earlier in Cincinnati the big ship was owned by rivals of the company said to have purchased the right to transport released prisoners.

It would clear up a very sticky situation, officials agreed, to put *all* remaining prisoners aboard the *Sultana*.

Even in this period of lax inspection, builders were issued certificates specifying load limits. Launched as a freighter whose cargo was to have been long-staple cotton from the Mississippi delta, the *Sultana* could not legally transport more than 376 passengers and crew members. A bigger load would automatically demand forced-firing of the four big tubular boilers, and every riverman knew that too much steam was worse than none.

There was no pretense at even the most perfunctory enforcement of regulations. It was all-important to quash stories about bribery before someone in Washington launched an investigation.

"Everybody goes on the *Sultana*! Everybody goes this trip!"

Word spread rapidly through Vicksburg and surrounding

27

camps. Union veterans swarmed to the riverbank in a special train. Others came by wagon and on foot.

For a few hours after loading began, officers tried to keep rolls. Then the restless, home-hungry surge of humanity proved too great. Men pushed past clerks, ignored sections designated for Ohio, Michigan, Indiana, and other states, and stopped wherever they could find standing room.

By the time the main refugee camp and satellite camps around it were empty, nearly every square foot of the *Sultana* was occupied. No one could give an accurate head count. Testimony given at an official inquiry indicated that the best that could be offered was an educated guess: 2300 to 2500 veterans, 75 to 100 civilian passengers, and a crew of 80.

In the entire history of the mighty Mississippi no comparable company of men had ever been assembled on one ship.

Launch time was delayed by the necessity of making some quick repairs to the steam lines leading from one of the boilers. But when this work was done, the big ship had enough power to move upstream against the current. Her destination was Cairo, Illinois, the debarkation point for men who had been prisoners of war.

As the *Sultana* left the wharf, captains of two other steamers registered protests with military officers. Both the *Carroll* and the *Gay* were ready to go, they explained. Neither ship was fully loaded. Each could have taken three or four hundred men. But their requests to transport some of the ex-prisoners had been rejected.

Since she lay so deep in the water, the steamer chosen for the big evacuation job moved more slowly than usual. It took her more than seventeen hours to reach Memphis, where she docked shortly after 7:00 P.M. on April 26.

Coal bins were being emptied much faster than usual; the supply of fuel had to be replenished. Except for a consignment of a hundred hogsheads of sugar, there was no freight for Memphis. Idle soldiers, glad to get off the crowded decks and stretch their legs a bit, volunteered to help crew members roll the barrels off.

Many men went ashore to buy drinks in the notorious Whiskey Chute. George Downey of the 9th Indiana Cavalry asked directions to the telegraph office. He needed money from home in order to make final stages of his journey after disembarking at Cairo.

Downey expected a quick reply, but didn't get it. While he waited in hope of receiving a remittance, the *Sultana* moved out into the river.

Downey spent his last $2 to hire a boatman to row him to the Arkansas side of the river, where the steamer was due to stop long enough to pick up another thousand bushels of coal.

Back on the ship, the Indiana native managed to find two men he knew. He told them of his adventure, exulted at his good luck in catching the boat, and rolled up in his blanket to go to sleep.

By then he and more than one thousand of his comrades had less than an hour to live.

Stripped to their waists, stokers worked in shifts. Orders had come to "pour on the coal, and keep this thing moving." There was a rumor, never confirmed but plausible, that the chief engineer had wired safety valves in place so that every available ounce of steam pressure could be applied to the churning side wheels.

Midnight came and passed. At intervals the big steamer shuddered as the speed of currents racing toward the Gulf of Mexico increased a trifle. Straining with all her might against the Father of Waters, loaded far beyond capacity, and pushing to the limits of her endurance, the *Sultana* blew up shortly before or after 2:00 A.M. on April 27.

Investigation suggested, but did not prove beyond doubt, that the #3 boiler went first. Fragments of hot metal from it ripped and tore through the heart of the ship. Then two more boilers exploded.

Many passengers were killed in their sleep. Some died from the blast. Others were crushed by falling timbers. Almost in the fashion of a scene depicted in a slow-motion picture, half of the steamer fell apart.

Men not killed in the explosion were in the turbulent water before they knew what had happened.

Noise of the explosion was heard all the way to Memphis. There the watch hand aboard the gunboat U.S.S. *Grosbeak* insisted on arousing his skipper. On the assumption that only the *Sultana* could have produced so loud a noise, the *Grosbeak* was ordered into action. Other steamers, smaller and closer to the site of the disaster, moved as rapidly as they could against the strong current in order to save survivors.

Many might have been saved had it not been for fire. Flames licked the timbers of the disemboweled vessel. Then gusts of wind pushed the fire toward survivors clustered together on the bow of the drifting hulk. It gave a lurch and big smokestacks toppled over.

Men who jumped into icy water found it hard to keep afloat. A few crowded onto a hastily improvised raft.

Sgt. William Fies, whose left arm was mangled, rode to safety on a board. He shared it with a fellow refugee until his comrade, whose name he never learned, became numb and fell off. More than an hour later Fies seized branches of a cottonwood sapling and pulled himself to dry ground.

No one knew the number of the dead. There were no records from which to notify next of kin.

A death barge made daily round trips from Memphis to the site of the explosion. Each time it was loaded with bodies of burned, crushed, and drowned men who had spent months in prison and thought they were getting close to their homes.

Attempts at fixing the blame led nowhere.

Captain Nate Wintringer, second engineer, got out alive. His license was revoked in Washington, but no notice of this action was sent to the St. Louis customs inspectors. As a result Wintringer's license was routinely renewed when it came due. Wintringer, whose duties gave him immediate supervision of the boiler room, even published a newspaper notice saying that "he was off watch when the unfortunate incident occurred."

At the time, newspapers and magazines gave hardly more than passing attention to the tragedy that took more lives than the 1,400 persons lost in the 185 steamboat explosions prior to 1850.

On April 29, the *New York Times* ran a five-inch story, one column wide. *Harper's Weekly* published a vivid sketch on May 20 but made no attempt to delve into the tragedy or to suggest ways to prevent its recurrence.

Lincoln had been shot on April 14. Andrew Johnson assumed the presidency on the fifteenth. General Joseph E. Johnston surrendered to Sherman on the twenty-sixth and brought armed resistance of the Confederacy to an end. On the same day, John Wilkes Booth died in a Virginia barn.

Numb from this mind-jolting series of events, men and women of the day largely ignored the *Sultana* and her victims.

Not until the 1890's, when the full story of that terrible night first began to be retold in depth, were there any constructive results. Great numbers of steamers still plied the Mississippi and her tributaries. Pushed into action by the tragedy that had occurred almost three decades earlier Congress enacted legislation requiring all passenger-carrying vessels on inland waterways to use boilers with built-in safety features. Too much steam, said the spirit of this lifesaving legislation, is worse than no steam at all.

*September 1, 1894*
*Hinckley, Minnesota*

# 5 Jim Root's Race with the North Woods

Air pollution was not considered a problem in 1894. Few persons had so much as conceived the idea that it might one day become a problem. Settlers trickling into the great forests of Minnesota kept "clearing fires" going for days on end as they got rid of trees and brush removed from the land. Smoke was considered to be a sign of progress. On most dry days it could be seen and smelled almost anywhere in the state.

That is one reason citizens of the sawmill town of Hinckley paid little attention to the blue haze they saw when they got up on the morning of September 1, 1894.

Promptly at seven o'clock the whistle of the big Brennan Lumber Co., largest employer in the whole region, blew to announce that another day's work was starting. So much lumber went out that the remote town was linked with St. Paul and Duluth not merely by one railroad, but by two competing ones.

At the Eastern Minnesota Railroad depot a freight train stood ready to depart with its cargo of green lumber. Later in the day passenger trains would come both to this station and to that of the St. Paul & Duluth Railroad. How important those trains would become no one dreamed during midmorning hours.

Blue-gray haze became so dense that payroll clerks at the sawmill had to light kerosene lamps. A sudden burst of wind whipped flames from an old logging road and sparks reached outskirts of town. There were half a dozen calls, each to a different site, but the volunteer fire department had no difficulty bringing these blazes under control.

Shortly after 1:00 p.m. the situation changed.

A telegraph message from the south reported that nearby Pokegama was "burning furiously and the town could not be saved." By now, grayish clouds were turning black.

Father Lawler, the only Catholic priest in the logging town, decided to take matters in his own hands. Waving his arms he ran up and down main streets of the village shouting in his deep bass voice: "Forest fire! Run! Everybody run!"

Many struck out for the shallow river at the edge of town. Others headed for the big gravel pit, always holding a few feet of muddy water. At least seventy-five hurried to the Eastern Minnesota Railroad station where a passenger train had joined the still-waiting freight.

Youthful Ernest Stephen, M.D., begged townsfolk to hurry. At his insistence, railroaders hastily switched and coupled the two trains together. As the last of the refugees boarded, paint on the railroad cars began to blister.

William Best and Ed Barry, at the throttles of the two locomotives, headed out of town picking up speed as fast as their heavy load permitted. Just as they crossed the bridge over Grindstone River, its creosote-soaked timbers burst into flame. More refugees were waiting there, waving for help.

Best and Barry didn't dare stop, but they did slow down enough to enable runners to catch the train and jump aboard. With an estimated two hundred desperate men, women, and children crowded into two passenger cars plus a baggage car and caboose, the hybrid train roared into Sandstone village, eight miles to the north.

Refugees shouted word of their plight, reported that "Pokegama has gone up in smoke," and offered to make room for others. Old-time loggers, who with their families made up the

33

entire population of Sandstone, shook their heads. They had lived through many warnings of forest fires.

Not a person in Sandstone joined the party of refugees. After a brief pause the motley train moved on north. Twenty minutes later fire destroyed every structure in Sandstone.

Back in Hinckley, those who had run to the Grindstone River found that water was too shallow to give protection except in occasional deeper pools. At the gravel pit the situation was even worse.

Singly and by families, persons who decided they couldn't survive if a real forest fire swept over their places of refuge took to the railroad tracks. Alternately walking briskly, then trotting until they were out of breath, they headed north toward what they hoped would prove a place of safety.

Jim Root, at the throttle of Engine #4, had pulled out of Duluth shortly after two o'clock. He was on a limited run— operating a fast train that was scheduled to make only a few stops on the way to St. Paul.

Visibility became very poor before he had been out of Duluth fifteen minutes. Root turned on the headlight of his locomotive and leaned forward in order to scan the track ahead.

Two miles north of Hinckley station, he turned to fireman Jack McGowan. "We may not make it," he said. "There's plenty of wind behind that big fire to the south."

Just then he caught sight of a tousle-haired boy, running barefoot along the tracks. Behind him were desperate men, women, and children all fleeing for their lives.

"Hinckley's burning!" one refugee blurted. "Half the town's dead!"

Root stopped his train and ordered passengers to make room for refugees. Within minutes nearly one hundred pushed aboard. Molly McNeil, sixteen, was the last to make it.

"Can't get to Hinckley," she panted to the brakeman. "Trestle over Grindstone River already on fire."

Word was relayed to Jim Root, a veteran railroader with a hankering to set a speed record. He pondered a moment, then gave a long blast and threw his engine into reverse. The nearest water was at Skunk Lake, six miles back up the line. Already Root could see flames leaping through treetops.

A steady twenty-mile wind was pushing the fire. At times it gained fresh momentum from its own heat. Leaping and twirling it darted like a frenzied demon. Engine #4 had hardly picked up speed before a blast of superheated air caught up with it.

Jim Root had turned sideways on his seat. That act probably saved his life, for every pane of glass in his locomotive was shattered simultaneously. Flying fragments tore into his neck, shoulders, and forehead. Many windows in the coaches were smashed. Crossties blazed on both sides of the track, and the baggage car caught fire.

Wiping blood from his eyes the engineer leaned far out the window in a futile attempt to see where he was going. Then the fire-demon pounced on the unprotected cab with all its fury. Root gasped and slumped over his hot throttle, unconscious. His shirt blazed, and the grimy side-curtains disappeared in a burst of flame.

Jack McGowan, shielded from the worst of the blast, was not injured. He grabbed a bucket and began dipping water from the tank of the locomotive.

As Root regained consciousness he instinctively peered at the steam gauge. "God!" he moaned. "Just ninety-five pounds!"

Shifting the throttle to full open, he sent the train hurtling backward. It swayed and bucked, but gave no indication of leaving the tracks.

Flames, meanwhile, appeared to be almost deliberately chasing the fleeing train. Flames scurried along inside woodwork of the cab. Big blisters appeared on painted surfaces. Even coal in the tender caught fire.

Root's hands swelled so much that the skin became tight and he could hardly bend his fingers. Each fresh blast from the pursuing inferno knocked him off his seat. He crawled back so often that he lost count.

Each time, McGowan threw water on him. Between forays into the front of the cab, the fireman retreated to his shelter and periodically emptied the bucket over his own head.

Accustomed to perils of what was then backwoods country, many passengers took the situation calmly. C. A. Vandever, of Davenport, Iowa, tried to calm the conductor who seemed crazed by the heat. Dr. W. H. Crary, of St. Paul, used his

35

prescription pad to jot down notes until the paper caught fire. He estimated that when flames reached a growth of tall pines they leaped through the trees at 80 miles per hour.

Some passengers lost control of themselves. Molly McNeil saw one man kiss his wife and then jump through a window. Two elderly Chinese, crouched near an open door, refused to move to a safer spot. They burned to death where they knelt.

Half sobbing, Jim Root wiped his eyes. He could not see more than four feet beyond the track, but landmarks indicated that the train had reached Skunk Lake. It ground to a halt, with fires blazing in every car. There was no opportunity—or need—to attempt an explanation. Frenzied passengers piled off and ran for the shallow water.

It was protected by a barbed-wire fence.

With bare hands, men ripped wire from posts. Then almost three hundred persons plunged into slimy water seldom more than eighteen inches deep.

Engineer Jim Root was too far gone to make it by himself. McGowan and two other men pulled Root's hands from the throttle, gasping as they found that all the skin had stayed on the iron.

His eyebrows were burned off. Most of his hair was gone. His entire face was a mass of livid blisters.

There seemed little hope that he could live, but the fireman insisted on dragging him to the edge of the pond. Dawn found him breathing but unconscious—unable to see the twisted iron that constituted remains of his crack limited scattered along the track.

Root eventually recovered. The official death list, which was not compiled until late November, indicated a count of 418 dead in Hinckley and half a dozen surrounding villages. Many were buried in a mass grave, marked by a plaque that is dedicated to "The Pioneers of Civilization in the Forests of Minnesota."

There is no bronze marker commemorating the feat of engineer Jim Root. He died in obscurity and never established a high-speed mark in any classification.

But the now-forgotten hero set a record that has never been

matched. Guiding his stricken train backward at an estimated eighteen miles per hour, Jim Root saved fifty lives for each of the six miles of the trip. His race against fire, familiar only to a handful of railroad buffs, has no equal in the saga of the iron horse.

*July 4, 1898*
*Waters off Nova Scotia*

# 6 Last Voyage of La Bourgogne

The passenger liner *La Bourgogne*, operated by the French Compagnie Generale Transatlantique, was rammed by the British steel bark *Cromartyshire* about 5:00 A.M. on Independence Day, 1898. The vessels collided in a dense fog at a spot about sixty miles south of Sable Island. Part of the Canadian province of Nova Scotia, the island is an exposed sandbar about one mile wide and twenty miles long. Linked with more than two hundred marine disasters, the island was long famous as "the graveyard of the Atlantic."

Captain Jean-Paul Deloncle was well acquainted with dangers of the region. But when he encountered heavy fog, he placed schedule above safety. As a result, only 165 persons out of the crew and passenger list of the French vessel lived to describe their experiences. All 560 who died in icy waters could have been saved if captains of the two vessels had relied upon ship-to-ship radio communication in lieu of time-honored but clumsy signals.

*La Bourgogne,* noted for speedy crossing of the Atlantic in all kinds of weather, eased out of New York harbor on July 2; all aboard expected to reach Le Havre without trouble. In July there was no danger of encountering icebergs, but dense fog was hit when the big liner was just six hours out of port. Described as "inordinately proud of his place of command," Deloncle considered it a matter of honor to press forward on schedule.

German-born Oswald Kirkner, an ice-cream maker on Staten Island who occupied a second-class cabin, reported that "few of the passengers had crossed the Atlantic more than once, but even as amateurs most of us realized we were moving too fast. By mid-morning on July 3, visibility had dropped to forty yards. Still there were no indications that our captain intended to reduce speed."

Instead of lifting as it often did at that season, the fog grew more dense. By evening it was so thick that the pilot's visibility was reduced to less than twenty yards. With her heavy engines throbbing the liner plunged forward at a speed of about seventeen or eighteen knots—roughly equivalent to twenty miles per hour on land.

By midnight the vessel was more than 150 miles north of her normal course. Captain Deloncle paced the deck impatiently and insisted that "fog or no fog, we must make up for lost time." Even allowing for possible errors in navigation he was sure that the ship was too far south to hit Sable Island and join a host of other vessels in the graveyard of the sea.

Deloncle was right about Sable Island—but failed to reckon with the possibility of collision with another ship.

The *Cromartyshire*, powered by wind rather than steam, was inching its way forward through the fog at about four knots. Following long-established custom the sailing vessel sounded its foghorn at one-minute intervals. Mrs. Henderson, wife of the ship's captain, was the first to sense danger. "I got out of my bunk early," she said. "This was my custom when the weather was thick. Though I could see nothing, I heard a steamer's whistle blowing on the port side of our vessel. I called it to the attention of my husband, and he alerted the first mate.

"Suddenly the huge hull of an ocean greyhound loomed up in the mist going at least seventeen knots. Our signal system was hopelessly inadequate. Almost as soon as I caught the first glimpse of the big ship there was a fearful crash. I hurried to my cabin to dress our children, for I feared that our vessel would sink."

It was not until eight or ten minutes later that officers of both vessels realized that the sailing ship was barely damaged, while the bowsprit of the tiny *Cromartyshire* had sliced a huge chunk from the forward section of the big liner.

Fearful of litigation that could force the line into bankruptcy, owners of the stricken ship released only one official statement.

"Boat #1 was smashed. Then, dragging aft, the bowsprit of the British vessel damaged our #3 and #5 boats, broke in the starboard boiler hold and engine room. According to the purser's watch, the impact occurred at 5:10. Passengers were doubtless all below asleep. Before they could get on deck the ship had taken a heavy list to starboard. This made it impossible to launch the port boats.

"The officers' boat, #7 on the starboard side, succeeded in pushing off. Then the funnel fell in and crushed it. Since the purser's watch stopped when he was thrown into the water at 5:50, the whole time from the collision until she sank must have been less than forty minutes."

Matter of fact language of the formal statement disguises the real story. No explanation for the dangerous speed and the movement off course was ever offered. Gustav Grimaux, a French passenger, said that there never was anything approaching an orderly attempt to evacuate the doomed vessel.

"Many of the passengers knew nothing at all about the sea," according to Grimaux. "One party of at least forty women rushed into a port-side lifeboat that moved farther and farther away from launch position as the liner settled. A few of them scrambled out at the last minute and jumped into the water, but most went down with the ship."

Charles Duttwellers, a German, got into a boat that was tied fast to the ship. When he realized that it was certain death to remain any longer he jumped. Later he told reporters: "I was carried down in the whirlpool made by the sinking steamer. When I had been in the water about half an hour a boat came within reach. I held up my hand for rescue and attempted to grasp the side of the boat. Wretches in it shoved me off with boathooks, and my left eye was badly cut.

"I saw women shoved away from boats with oars and boathooks. Members of the crew assaulted many passengers with any implement that came handy. If no instrument was to be had they punched the men and women helpless in the water with their fists."

Eventually rescued by a small boat from the *Cromartyshire*, Duttweller's story might have been considered biased had it not been supported by many other survivors. John Burgi, who was especially solicitous about his aged mother, succeeded in placing her near the middle of a lifeboat a few minutes before *La Bourgogne* went down.

"Sailors fighting for their own lives threw my poor old mother into a watery grave," Burgi said. "They threw me out of the boat five times. Then they beat me with oars and shoved me under the boat. I managed to stay afloat for nine hours and was finally rescued by a party from the vessel that had rammed the liner."

Though the bow of the *Cromartyshire* was damaged, she took aboard as many survivors as could be found. Then the Allan liner *Grecian* towed the British vessel sixty miles north to Sable Island.

All senior officers of the stricken liner went down with Captain Deloncle and the ship. But of the 165 survivors about one hundred were members of the crew and four were subaltern officers. The passenger list included nearly three hundred women—but only one of them lived to tell of her experiences. She was the wife of Prof. A. D. Lacasse, a language teacher in the school system of Plainfield, N. J. Lacasse was the only saloon passenger on deck at the time of impact. He raced below, aroused his wife, and led her to the deck. Holding hands, the two jumped simultaneously. Eventually both found places on a crude raft that swirled and tilted when *La Bourgogne* sank.

August Pourgi, one of the passengers who made it to shore, declared that "from beginning to end, the whole business was a lasting disgrace to the French merchant marine. Instead of taking normal precautions, the captain acted as though the world would come to an end if we did not reach Le Havre exactly on schedule. Moving through dense fog at high speed with no ship-to-ship communication except horns and whistles, disaster was inevitable once the two vessels chanced to embark on a collision course."

Though Pourgi was a landsman, veterans of the sea agreed with his verdict. It was imperative, said both French and British officials, to devise some system of communication more rapid and precise than flags by day and horns by night.

Four years earlier Guglielmo Marconi had succeeded in "telegraphing without wires" over a distance of just thirty feet. Once the principles of wireless were developed, prograss was rapid. Marconi's electromagnetic signals were successfully transmitted over a distance of almost two miles in February, 1896.

The inventor went to England in search of financial backing and took out his basic British patent on June 2, 1896—two years before the disastrous collision on the other side of the Atlantic. At the time La Bourgogne went down, wireless messages were being transmitted from stations twenty-five miles away from receiving sets.

In the U. S., public absorption with the Spanish-American War was so great that loss of a passenger liner with more than twice the casualties of the battleship Maine was largely ignored. Not so in England and in Europe. Spurred by the disaster that might have been averted by use of Marconi's wireless, on January 7, 1904, the Marconi Company formally adopted CQD as the international radio distress signal. Two years later at the International Radio Telegraphic Convention in Berlin, CQD was supplemented by another signal that soon superseded it—SOS.

Just five years after La Bourgogne took hundreds of persons to their death, Captain Ludwig Arnson of the Red Star liner Kroonland saved his ship and his passengers by broadcasting a call for help. Once ships began to be equipped with instruments for transmitting and receiving code messages by wireless, it was a relatively short step to the biggest lifesaving device in the history of the sea: ship-to-ship radio.

More than any other single event, the needless tragedy of July 4, 1898, involving a vessel whose name is familiar to few present-day travelers, spurred development of fast and accurate communication between vessels on the high seas.

*September 8, 1900*
*Galveston, Texas*

# 7 Galveston Tidal Wave

Colonel Michael B. Menard, a pioneer developer of real estate, took a plunge in December, 1836. For $50,000—a colossal sum in that era—he purchased from the Republic of Texas "one league and one labor" (three statute miles plus 177.14 acres) of land on the east end of then-deserted Galveston island.

Within five years Menard had formed a joint stock company with the purpose of making Galveston the chief port of entry for goods flowing into and out of the entire southwest.

Galveston Bay Bridge, completed in 1860, formed the land leg of what founders had envisioned as one of the world's great transportation centers. The first train ran over lines of the Galveston, Houston, and Henderson R.R. weeks after completion of the bridge.

Meanwhile construction crews worked double shifts to complete the first set of docks. They received so much heavy cargo that the federal government set about to improve the harbor.

Originally obstructed by an inner bar over which the depth of water was only nine and a half feet and an outer bar with

43

just twelve feet of water, Galveston harbor could not accommodate the new breed of ocean liners.

To remedy this situation a complex system of jetties was devised. Sandstone riprap was covered with granite blocks weighing from five to twelve tons each. When finished, the south jetty measured 35,603 feet in length and the north jetty stretched for 25,907 feet.

Both jetties were built at a height of five feet above mean low tide and were twelve to fifteen feet in width at the top. At the shore the two massive structures were two miles apart. Slowly converging, their tips were about 7,000 feet apart.

This plan had the effect of containing, or confining, water. More water meant a much greater tidal scour, cutting a channel for deep-sea ships. By 1899, engineers congratulated themselves on having succeeded in securing a depth of about twenty-six feet of water at mean low tide on both bars.

The result was a constantly accelerating flow of bigger and bigger ships. These, in turn, provided an economic base for mushroom growth in the city of Galveston. More than half of the city's expanding business and residential area was approximately at sea level. Hundreds of homes, plus numerous warehouses and factories, were built with their ground floors two, three, and even five feet below sea level.

Judge William P. Ballinger did not like this state of affairs.

On August 20, 1886, a storm swept down upon the city and did considerable damage. As a result, Judge Ballinger on August 28 addressed "an open letter to the citizens of Galveston."

"I do not need to tell any but the newest newcomers that our city is built on an island," the jurist said. "About thirty miles in length, the entire north side of the island fronts on Galveston Bay. But the entire south side fronts on the Gulf of Mexico.

"In years since the city was incorporated in 1839, there have been six major storms. None has caused substantial loss of life, though each has been a source of both inconvenience and damage to property.

"I cannot too strongly urge the *vulnerability* of this fair city, if hit by a tropical storm of the first magnitude. Thirteen years ago the Constitution of the State of Texas granted to all coun-

44

ties and cities bordering on the coast of Mexico the right to issue bonds and to construct breakwaters, or sea-walls.

"We must take advantage of this provision now," Judge Ballinger concluded. "Next year may be too late."

There was a lively discussion in newspapers, but no steps were taken to act upon the judge's plea.

All went well until September 8, 1900.

That day a terrific hurricane from the West Indies sent huge waves dashing over the port that citizens had come to label "the oleander city."

There had been a few terse warnings from the weather bureau: "Heavy swells—rising wind and tide likely." "Advise seeking secure place for the night."

Few citizens of Galveston took the warnings seriously. After all, they were accustomed to sporadic bursts of high wind nearly every summer and fall. Since no point within the city limits was more than six feet above sea level, flooding was taken for granted as an inevitable fact of life—inconvenient, but not dangerous.

By midafternoon on the fateful day, however, the mood of citizens changed. A steadily falling barometer caused skippers of big oceangoing vessels to double-check straining cables. Many shops and offices closed by 3:30.

Until then no one had seriously considered flight to the mainland. At first there was a mere trickle, then a stream of humanity as dock workers, members of ships' crews, housewives, children, and youths decided to abandon the city that seemed certain to be hit by high water.

Surging tides moved faster than people, however. Street by street, the city was assaulted and then captured by the pounding sea. Utility plants were out of commission, so there were no lights to aid stragglers when dusk fell.

Precisely at 7:32 P.M., as winds reached hurricane levels, a vast tidal wave roared out of the Gulf of Mexico. Water trapped between arms of the jetties exploded over Galveston in a twelve-foot wave of carnage.

Buildings toppled. Big steamers were tossed far over the docks into the business section of the city. Tombstones fell by the

45

score; surging water scoured away earth and brought up dozens of coffins to float madly about the stricken city.

Though only one wave was measured at twelve feet, dozens of smaller ones pounded and hammered as they rumbled, white-crested, over ruins of the port that had been bustling with activity a few hours earlier.

Destruction worked by the storm king on September 8 shocked the civilized world. Property losses were conservatively estimated at $17,000,000—one of the biggest tolls taken by a natural disaster up to that time. Far worse, more than 6,000 persons were dead.

Several books have been written about the Galveston tidal wave, and most volumes dealing with major disasters devote a chapter to it. Practically all stop with a detailed account of destruction and carnage worked by the cruel sea.

But the real story of the Galveston disaster centers in human response to what seemed at first an overwhelming defeat of man by forces of nature.

A few merchants abandoned their ruined property and made fresh starts elsewhere. Owners of one shipping line forbade their captains to use Galveston as a port of call—then relented because no other city on the southwestern coast could accommodate the biggest ocean liners.

Even in the case of families with only one or two survivors, most Galveston folk decided to stick it out—and to fight back.

As one by-product of the storm the city was left with a channel thirty feet deeper than it had been on September 7. To protect that channel—and the city to which it led—citizens built a gigantic seawall whose top was more than twelve inches above the crest of 1900's storm waters.

In the city the ground level was raised by pumping in millions of tons of sand from the floor of the Gulf of Mexico. This meant that telephone poles, streetcar tracks, and those buildings not leveled by the storm had to be raised as much as seventeen feet.

"Galveston, most mercilessly battered by the cruel sea, has refused to capitulate," a newspaper editorial exulted. "Our motto has become, 'Attack the enemy!' We must conquer the sea; we shall conquer the sea."

It took four years to complete the seawall, but when finished it shielded the port city from fourteen-foot waves generated by the hurricane of 1911. This time property damage was in the range of four million dollars—and only twelve lives were lost. Galveston refused to be counted out. Her comeback against the raging sea, lauded in many ballads and songs, made the city a lasting inspiration to every community stricken by catastrophe so stunning that the initial reaction is to abandon all efforts at recovery and rebuilding.

# 8 Panic in the Iroquois Theater

Most persons who achieve brief or lasting fame for having saved lives of others have known precisely how many they rescued. Not so Eddie Foy.

Born in 1857 as plain Edward Fitzgerald, he took Eddie Foy as his stage name when he began to break into the big time as a comedian. By 1903 he had already won international fame for his performances in *Cinderella or the Crystal Slipper*.

His reputation and personal magnetism helped to pack Chicago's palatial Iroquois Theater for most performances of an elaborate pantomime called *Mr. Bluebeard*.

Foy went into the bargain-price matinee on the next to last day of the year as a famous comedian. He emerged as one of the all-time heroes of the stage.

"No one has the faintest idea of how many lives Eddie Foy saved," said Chicago's building commissioner George Williams. "Five or six hundred is a good, round figure. It could have been a few less than that—or many more.

"Foy didn't get a medal; he refused to be nominated for one.

But because he risked his own life by going to center stage, front, he reduced the toll in the worst theater fire this country has ever seen."

Still not fully recovered from the great fire of 1871, Chicago's civic leaders and builders were often ultracautious. Many of the buildings erected in the Windy City during the quarter century after the Great Fire were decades ahead of those in other urban centers.

That's why the huge Iroquois Theater was billed as "fireproof."

Builders employed a great deal of marble, plus vast sections of plate glass—not yet generally accepted by U. S. architects. Mahogany walls and flowing staircases were flammable, but experts who inspected the building pronounced it "one of the safest in the world." In the event that there should be a fire, owner-manager Harry J. Powers proudly pointed out, "There are thirty exits. That's twice as many as would be needed to empty the building in a matter of minutes!"

Eight tragic minutes on the afternoon of December 30, 1903, proved the experts to be wrong. The virtually fireproof building was crammed with highly flammable material and it was packed with panic-prone patrons, who found most of the thirty exits locked when they raced to open them.

*Mr. Bluebeard*, brought from England complete with thousands of yards of drops earlier used in London's big Drury Lane Theater, opened at the nearly new Iroquois on November 23.

From its first performance the play was a hit.

Visitors from out of town were almost as impressed with the playhouse as they were with the play. The Iroquois had a huge promenade foyer that resembled something from a European palace. Distance from floor to ceiling was sixty feet, with grand staircases ascending on both sides of the house.

Patrons sitting in the 1600 plush seats craned their necks to peer at the rococo gilding above, murmuring in admiration as they studied the profusion of drops hanging over the stage.

Wednesday afternoon was a special performance aimed at the boys and girls whose Christmas holiday would soon be over. Performer Annabelle Buchan, who played the role of Stella, queen of the fairies, later estimated that 80 percent of the audience was made up of children accompanied by their mothers.

Even though the thermometer stood at –8°, the performance was a sellout long before curtain time. Managers later admitted having dispensed "about one hundred standing-room tickets." Expert witnesses who testified at the coroner's inquest challenged that figure, estimating that about four hundred standees crowded every aisle and exit.

So many stage settings had to be handled that the crew of stagehands was much larger than usual—at least 150. With approximately 250 members of the cast added to the total, the fateful afternoon saw the Iroquois packed with about 2,400 patrons, performers, and workers.

No one showed the least concern. It was public knowledge that the theater had been pronounced fireproof after careful examination by experts.

Throughout the first act of *Mr. Bluebeard* everything went perfectly.

Soon after the second act began, a double octette—eight men and eight women—moved to the center of the huge stage. Their number was called "In the Pale Moonlight." In order to create the desired mood, it was necessary to flood the stage with bluish light.

An electrician stationed on a small platform operated two high-temperature carbon lamps that helped to create the effect of moonlight. Immediately after he turned on those lamps, according to later testimony, heat seared a painted canvas wing hidden from view of the audience.

Seconds later the flimsy piece burst into flame. Tongues of fire raced toward gauze drops and muslin backings. Because the operator of the carbon lamps gave no alarm and made no attempt to put out the fire, he was later charged with criminal negligence.

By the time stagehands below noticed what was happening, the proscenium drape was blazing. A few men tried to put out the fire. One grabbed a fire extinguisher but found it held no liquid that could be squirted on flames overhead. Eddie Foy, who was standing nearby, said that the extinguisher held "some kind of powder."

Another stagehand seized a long stick used as a lance in one scene, tried to beat out flames, then stood helplessly below when he found he could not reach them.

By now tongues of fire had begun to dart along tinderlike strips of fabric transformed into scenery by use of oil-base paints. Ropes, cords, and twine above the center of the stage gave that area an appearance several performers had already compared with a tropical forest. Precisely 280 drops—all flimsy, all flammable, all hanging where gusts of air could reach them—were neatly arranged. Without use of them, producers would have found it impossible to convey "the lavish look" that advertisements stressed in urging lovers of the theater to see *Mr. Bluebeard.*

Gauze and lace segments of the drops flared briefly, igniting the entire mass of fabric.

Still wearing tights and comic shoes, a short smock, and a wig from which a pigtail curved upward, the star of the show raced into the audience. Eddie Foy found his son Bryan, six, and hustled him into a mass of performers and stagehands already headed for nearby rear exits.

Then the man who had made his reputation as a clown ran to the center of the stage, far out on the apron that projected toward the audience whose members were still generally unaware of what had happened.

Eddie Foy signaled for Herbert Dillea, leader of the orchestra, to play.

"An overture!" Foy shouted. "Something good and loud! For God's sake, play! Play, play, and keep playing!"

A few musicians had already slipped from their seats. Most remained and responded to Dillea's gestures.

Instinctively clowning, Eddie Foy already had most of the audience laughing. Those who knew the story of *Mr. Bluebeard* assumed that new stage business had been inserted for the children's matinee.

"My one thought was, 'God help us to keep calm,' " Foy said in one of his rare statements about the fearful day. "I had every reason to believe the theater wouldn't burn—at least not very rapidly. So I tried to keep attention of the audience in order to prevent a stampede."

Simultaneously, Foy signaled insistently to stage hands. They

51

understood his gestures and obeyed. Down tumbled the fire-proof curtain that would shield the auditorium from flames on stage. One of the most expensive accessories of the Iroquois because it was made of then-new asbestos, that curtain was listed near the top of fire-preventive devices that enabled its owner to bill the theater as fireproof.

Down the costly curtain tumbled—until it was caught by a rope. With open doors behind the stage admitting icy air from outside, this arrangement of the curtain transformed the stage itself into a crude chimney through which smoke, sparks, and then flames swirled with fast-growing power.

Hundreds of patrons responded to Eddie Foy, who by this time was shouting pleas that they remain in their seats. Others turned their backs on the comedian and the orchestra and began a frenzied rush toward the rear of the vast building.

Once they got there, they discovered that only a few of the exits offered avenues to safety. Many were unmarked and un-lighted. A few were frozen or rusted shut so firmly that no amount of pushing would cause them to yield. Investigation after the tragedy revealed that several were locked.

Ushers gave no help. Because adolescent boys could be hired at rates below those demanded by experienced men, most ushers were high school juniors and seniors picking up a few dollars during the holidays.

Fear-maddened women in the balcony finally found one door they could open. By then the steps were swathed with flames spurting from an exit at a lower level.

Painters working across a narrow court from the Iroquois threw a ladder to the balcony that by now was jam-packed with panic-stricken women and children. One patron started across the ladder, then screamed as it wobbled crazily and tossed him to the street below.

Finally a big plank pushed across by the painters offered a narrow road to safety. Intense cold and the awkwardness of persons not accustomed to height slowed movements so much that only a dozen persons ever got across that lifesaving plank.

Stairways leading from the second balcony were jammed before the hundreds who had responded to Eddie Foy realized the theater was on fire. Especially at turns in stairways, bodies piled so high that some near the bottom were smothered or crushed to death. Heel prints on upturned faces of the dead gave eloquent testimony to the fact that when humans panic they are as dangerous as stampeding cattle.

Chicago's chief fire marshal, William Musham, was on the scene in less than two minutes after he heard the first belated alarm. Musham had gained fame in 1871. Then foreman of Little Giant Engine #6, it was he who directed the first stream of water used against the fire that is traditionally ascribed to a lantern overturned by Mrs. O'Leary's cow.

Musham sent in firemen to rescue any persons still alive and personally directed hose crews who ran their lines inside the Iroquois. They found no large flames and quickly put out all the small ones.

Eight terrible minutes after the first burst of flame was noticed, the fire was tapped out.

There is no certainty that anyone was killed by the flames. Scores of persons perished from heat and from smoke inhalation. But the greatest toll was taken by panic.

Police Chief O'Neill took one look at the dead in gallery hallways, shuddered, and said victims looked "like a field of timothy grass blown flat."

By evening, there were more than five hundred bodies in the morgue. The final official toll was 586 identified plus four unidentified dead. "Had it not been for Eddie Foy's diversion of great numbers on the main floor of the theater, the death toll might have been twice as great," O'Neill said.

Investigation revealed that the fireproof Iroquois—which suffered little damage—was filled with highly flammable cloth and wooden stage equipment. There were no fire axes, no hoses connected to standpipes, no extinguishers that sprayed liquid. Passageways, promenades, and galleries included many abrupt turns. Few exits were clearly marked, and many were not in readiness for use.

Two days after the fire Eddie Foy and most of the other performers in *Mr. Bluebeard* left for a New York opening. They took with them nightmare memories of America's worst theater fire.

Not simply in Chicago, where nineteen theaters were inspected and closed within a week, but throughout the nation authorities took a close second look at "entertainment palaces." Hundreds were found hazardous. Many were remodeled; some were permanently closed.

Mandatory lighting of exit signs plus installation of fire extinguishers were ordered in most U.S. cities. Producers were forbidden to use flammable drops. Regulations governing width of corridors and aisles, as well as design of stairways, were revised.

Since the Iroquois there have been many more theater fires in the United States. None has claimed so many victims as the "fireproof" palace; none has produced a center-stage hero comparable to the man who was billed as a comedian.

*June 15, 1904*
*East River, New York City*

# 9 Sinking
# of the *General Slocum*

Ask a person in Mishawaka or Tuscaloosa or San Diego what he thinks about the General Slocum affair, and he's likely to respond: "Who's he?" But on any June 15th, go to the Lutheran Cemetery in Queens, New York City, and ask one of the schoolchildren bringing flowers for a vast grave.

Regardless of the words he may use, the child in Queens will answer that question by exclaiming that the last day of the steamer *General Slocum* was "just awful."

Authorities never did agree about the death toll in the world's worst excursion boat disaster. According to the U. S. Steamboat Inspection Service it was "only 938." The New York police department stuck firmly to a figure of 1,031. Many lists of disasters compromise with a report of "more than 1,000."

Except for the principal actors in the drama everyone who knew anything about it agreed that it needn't have happened. Everything, without exception, went wrong. Nothing, absolutely nothing, was right—nothing under human control, that is. The weather was marvelous—a blue and white day with plenty of sunshine and just enough breeze to add zest to an excursion. Pastor G. F. C. Haas headed the procession of chattering and laughing Sunday school children and parents. It had become a tradition in the big St. Mark's German Lutheran Church to charter the *General Slocum* for an annual Sunday school voyage and picnic.

Elderly Captain William Van Schaick should have stopped the line when his wooden vessel reached capacity. He liked to report successful cruises, though, so stood quietly by and permitted about 1,360 passengers to file aboard the thirteen-year-old ship.

Special emphasis had been placed on the 1904 outing. Parents who worshiped at the church on Sixth Street in Manhattan's East Side had made a real effort to "get the kids out this year." As a result even the kindergarten children were included. Less than half a dozen students in the kindergarten stayed home because of illness or family plans. All the others crowded happily aboard the steamer.

Moored at the foot of East Third Street, the *General Slocum* was praised as "the latest thing." It even had electric lights—something few other vessels on the East River could boast about. But in order to preserve a hint of the romantic past, the big ship was propelled by side wheels much like those used earlier on Mississippi River steamers.

Excited tots and older children, along with their mothers and aunts and teachers and about a dozen men, handed over tickets printed in German and English and bearing the date June 15, 1904.

Long before the last stragglers came aboard, even persons who knew little about ships were aware that the *General Slocum* was slowly dipping deeper into the water under the weight of her load.

Most crew members were former truck drivers and dock workers. Along with their officers they closed their eyes to danger and gestured to latecomers that they should hurry aboard.

This was the first in an incredible series of mistakes, blunders, and failures.

Measuring 250 feet in length and 70 feet in width, the big vessel could make 18 miles per hour under favorable circumstances. Without mention of overloading Captain Van Schaick remarked to the pastor of the doomed congregation that "we may be a few minutes late reaching the picnic grounds today."

As members of the German band began rendering thumping tunes, the excursion steamer with white sides and gay yellow smokestacks paddled briskly toward Hell Gate. The ultimate destination was Locust Point, just beyond Throg's Neck in the Bronx.

In violation of all safety regulations, a forward storeroom was cluttered with cans of oil. To make matters worse barrels filled with leftover excelsior from a shipment of crockery stood near the flammable liquid.

Just what happened in that room during the first few minutes of the fateful voyage authorities were never able to determine. Some evidence suggested that an oiler on the way to the engine room passed through with a flaming torch. Other witnesses supported the view that a green hand among the crew had lighted a lamp in the room then dropped the match.

Regardless of the precise set of circumstances that set off the blaze, a brisk fire was burning by the time the ship reached Eighty-third Street.

Official testimony included a sworn statement that Frank Perditsky, fourteen, had noticed smoke. Excited, he pushed his way into areas that passengers were forbidden to enter. Before he could be stopped, he found "a man with gold braid on his cap"—sufficient to identify the officer as Captain Van Schaick himself—and managed to blurt: "Sir, something's wrong! I just saw smoke coming out of the boiler room."

Van Schaick ordered the boy to "shut up and mind your own business," then pushed him into the arms of a steward who guided him back to the deck.

"Ed, maybe you'd better take a look," the captain suggested.

First mate Edward Flanagan, a former ironworker, took a seaman along with him. They quickly discovered that smoke actually was coming from the interior of the vessel. It was a storeroom deep in its body, however, that yielded the telltale odor. Everything was fine in the engine room.

In spite of hundreds of pages of testimony during a formal investigation some details were never established. One important question centered upon the fact that the room in which the fire started was locked when Flanagan and his companion traced the smoke to it.

They shook the door, but were unable to open it. Flanagan ran to get a key. When he returned and pulled the door open, inrushing air fed flames that already had rope, dunnage, and old barrels smoldering.

A fire hose stood nearby.

"Water!" Flanagan yelled, as he turned the nozzle toward the source of the flames.

Seconds later he stood helplessly as he stared at the hose and realized it was not yielding a drop of water. It was not until much later that Flanagan heard shipmates testify that the fire hose had never been used and had never been inspected.

"It could be the engine . . . ," Flanagan surmised.

A seaman raced to start the donkey engine that had been installed in order to add pressure to water in the fire system. The engine coughed, shuddered, and then began firing steadily.

Still no water from the hose.

By now a dozen members of the crew were at the scene of danger. Two of them uncoupled the hose in order to inspect it. When they did, a solid rubber washer dropped to the deck. It had been placed there when the ship was first outfitted "in order to prevent water from dripping from the fire hose."

With washer removed, hose reassembled, and donkey engine pumping, the valve was turned once more. This time water rushed forward with full force.

When pressure hit the ancient linen hose to which the nozzle was connected, the hose burst in a dozen places at once.

Any amateur could see that the fire was now out of control. So much smoke poured out that it was noticed from shore. A factory workman saw it and turned in a call to the fire department though he felt it wasn't necessary, since the burning ship could make a sharp turn and reach shore within five or six minutes at the speed she was going.

Alerted by the call, men of a nearby engine company slid down brass poles and urged their horses into a gallop. They turned down 138th Street, stopped the engine, and pulled the hose by hand to the end of the longest pier.

It was useless. The excursion vessel did not attempt to alter her course. Instead she churned briskly away, bow into the wind, as she continued on her way toward the picnic ground.

Captain Van Schaick later said that he felt "a moral responsibility not to risk setting buildings on fire." It only appeared that he was headed toward the picnic ground, he said. Actually, he had ordered the pilot to turn toward North Brother Island. "It would take us only a few minutes, and there were no buildings that would be threatened."

Alerted by the call from shore the fireboat *Zophar Mills* was already in chase—a full mile astern. The tugboats *John Wade* and *Walter Tracy* joined the rescue effort, but were at least three-quarters of a mile away.

As the flaming vessel neared the spot chosen by her captain, Pilot Van Wart fumbled badly. Consequently he missed the narrow stretch of sandy shore that would have given hope to some aboard. Unable to correct the error because of the clumsy steering apparatus, he watched helplessly as the *General Slocum* steamed directly against a rocky cove.

With the ship grounded, her blazing bow lay in shallow water. At the stern, where hundreds of terrified passengers had run, water was about thirty feet deep.

Still, adults tried to take reasonable precautions. They searched for and found the ship's ten lifeboats, but couldn't free them from the cables with which they were lashed in place.

By now panic had broken out. Children fought with one another for life preservers, which broke open and spilled fragments of cork over the decks. At the trial which followed it was found that granulated cork had been used as an economy measure. Regulations required solid blocks of cork, considerably heavier than the granulated form. Since these makeshift life preservers didn't come up to weight requirements, each of them was fitted with a seven-inch bar of cast iron.

Great numbers of persons jumped into turbulent water near the still-turning paddlewheels. With or without life preservers, most of them drowned at once.

On deck, numbers of children were trampled to death.

Then flames cut through supporting timbers and the decks collapsed. Hundreds of screaming victims were thrown into the

59

flaming bowels of the ship. Many of them, burned beyond recognition, were buried in a common grave.

By 11:30 A.M., just ninety minutes from the time the last passenger had boarded, the carnage was over.

Before midnight, more than 600 bodies were recovered. Delivery wagons and coal carts were pressed into service to supplement ambulances and hearses. Morgues throughout the Bronx were choked with victims.

Hundreds more were still in the water. Some had plunged so hard that they sank far down and were captured in silt and mud. Cannon brought from the Brooklyn Navy Yard were fired over the water; vibrations caused mud to release an additional fifty bodies.

A coroner's jury charged Captain Van Schaick and Mate Flanagan with manslaughter in the first degree. The same charge was leveled against the inspector responsible for checking the ship's fire-fighting equipment. Officers of the *General Slocum's* owner, the Knickerbocker Company, were also charged.

Van Schaick eventually drew a sentence of ten years at hard labor as a result of being judged guilty of criminal negligence.

All others went free.

President Theodore Roosevelt demanded drastic reform of the U. S. Steamboat Inspection Service and personally fired eighty-year-old Chief Inspector Dumont. Editorial comment in cities as distant as London fed the demand for adequate fire hoses, life preservers, lifeboats, and fire drills on all passenger-carrying vessels.

As a result, when flowers go on graves in the Lutheran Cemetery each June, they commemorate not only stupidity and death, but also one of the most sweeping sets of reforms in U. S. maritime history.

Though victims were buried long ago, the outcome of the tragedy is still felt. Excursion vessels, riverboats, ferries, and even family-owned pleasure craft are required to meet safety standards that were raised to new levels because owners and operators of the *General Slocum* failed to value life above operating costs.

*November 13-20, 1909*
*Cherry, Illinois*

# 10  The Cherry Mine Disaster

Assistant mine superintendent George Eddy, slightly built and mild-mannered, didn't seem like a person who would fight when ordinary persons gave up. Put to the test, he won over a patient monster that wouldn't quit—the blazing hell of a coal mine on fire.

Carelessness probably started it. Some workman, trying to get ahead of the game so he could sneak a smoke, piled hay too high on his cart that operated 300 feet below the surface. Something had gone wrong with the electric system of the mine operated by the St. Paul Company, so kerosine torches were hung in the tunnels. Brushing against one of them, the top bales of hay on the cart began to smolder.

Unaware that the loaded cart was on fire, the workman left it and turned back for more hay. By the time a mule driver smelled smoke about 1:15 P.M., roof timbers were blazing.

Even at that, survivors said later, it might have been possible to put out the fire had someone thought of cutting off the ventilating fans. No one did. So the breeze drove flames straight toward the main shaft.

Cherry Mine, mainstay of the town of 2,000 in which it was located, was just six years old—clean and dry. Fat pine beams made good braces, but were never intended to stop a fire.

Most miners were recent immigrants from Europe. Nearly half came from Italy and France. Others were Irish and Slavic.

There was little water and mule drivers did not know how to connect the hose. They yelled at one another in two or three languages, dropped the dry hose and ran to warn their comrades.

One group headed for the third vein, eighty yards below, where 185 men were digging. Others ran to find the four hundred miners on the second level. Since the first-level vein had played out long ago, it was deserted.

Smoke rolled through the main tunnels and drifted into side passages. At the shouts of mule drivers, miners began dropping their tools and running toward the sole exit—the main shaft.

Two cages were in operation there. Cables of the cages ran on opposite sides of a single drum. This meant that when one cage was raised the other was automatically lowered. Though sturdy, the system was slow and clumsy.

Power came from an engine room on the surface, thirty yards from the mouth of the shaft. Tubes ran from this room to each landing in the mine. Hand-operated air pumps were placed at all stopping points. In order to get the cage moved, a workman had to signal the engineer by giving the prescribed number of strokes with a pump. Passengers inside the cage had no way to make the bell ring in order to guide the operator.

John Bundy, the mine superintendent, came running at the first alarm. He sent six volunteers into the tunnels to help guide workers to safety. Those nearest the main shaft were herded toward it and four cageloads were drawn safely to the surface.

Then built-in clumsiness of the signal system played into hands of the fire. Confusing and contradictory orders reached the engine room as men pumped messages from several points simultaneously: "Hoist!" "Stop!" "Lower!" "Hoist!" "Stop!"

Bewildered, the engineer halted the cage on the bottom. He pulled out his watch and laid it on his desk. After ten minutes without another signal, he raised the cage. Eight dead men lay in the metal hulk, their clothes blazing. Meanwhile, a few had escaped by climbing up the elevator cables.

James Bundy and his rescue squad were among those trapped below. By now, the fan had been reversed in order to pull flames away from the main shaft. Racing 300 yards along powder-dry timbers the fire spread into the ventilation shaft.

Weakened supports cracked, then gave way. Still turning, the heavy fan crashed into the pit. Gasping and coughing, frantic men tried to claw their way up the cables but were thrown back by water from fire hoses aimed haphazardly into the shaft.

When the fire started, relief agencies later reported, 572 men were at work. Before the shafts were sealed, 184 escaped.

Now the fire was complete master of the mine. Flames filled both shafts and licked toward the surface. Under the direction of James Steele, a dynamite crew laid heavy charges.

They blew up the building that spanned the two shafts, then had steel rails laid across their tops. Heavy boards, piled with sand, completed the cap. There was a possibility that the red devil beneath could be smothered to death.

But wives and children, mostly stolid and unemotional, needed no explanation. Even before Steele made his first statement to reporters, they knew that it was practically impossible that any men trapped underground could live.

George Eddy, who had been in a remote second-level entry when the fire started, didn't know what was happening on the surface. By the time he smelled smoke, it was too late for him to reach the elevator.

Turning back from the main shaft, Eddy ran for the ventilation shaft in order to descend to the third level. On the way he met a stream of refugees. He tried to stop them, but most ignored his gestures and ran on toward the exit. A few turned to follow him.

Eddy decided they didn't have time to make it to the third level. He selected a side passage and guided his little band into it.

"No chance to get out, boys!" he panted. "We've got to seal ourselves in and let 'em come for us."

They had no explosives or tools.

Three big miners threw their weight against a sagging timber and knocked it down. Roof boards were pulled out and a cave-in followed. With bare hands they dug loose coal and shale from the walls and completed a thick barricade. Near the top Eddy shoved in a pick-handle in order to have a hole communicating with the outer tunnel.

When the first frenzy was over the refugees took stock. Twenty-one men and a mule, with no food or water. The chamber in which they were sealed was at least one hundred feet long and seemed to have plenty of oxygen.

Eddy and lieutenants he selected took charge of all the lamps and extinguished all but one.

Overhead, the stricken town was reached by one band of volunteers after another. Soon after daybreak they took off the cap and prepared to climb into the mine to bring out the dead.

Lacking masks and oxygen tanks they had to have air. A temporary fan was rigged over the ventilator shaft. But as soon as it started turning, smoke began pouring out the main shaft. Minutes passed, and instead of becoming lighter it grew black and dense. Then flames licked toward the surface. Cherry Mine was blazing more furiously than the day before.

This time, it was all the militia could do to hold back the mob pressing toward the entrance. Women who could restrain themselves at news their husbands were dead began to scream at the idea they would never recover their bodies. Grimy children, long since emptied of tears, stared without fully understanding what the new fire meant.

There was nothing to do but reseal the mine.

Refugee stations were opened in churches and lodge halls. Company officials began compiling the death list and announced that survivors would be paid $150 for each life lost. Relief agencies began seeking emergency funds. Ernest P. Bicknell, national director of the Red Cross, wired that he would arrive with a relief fund of $100,000.

Six carloads of coffins, bought at wholesale in Chicago, were rolling toward the stricken village. So were flat cars loaded with huge water tanks. The town's meager water supply wasn't big enough to douse the flames, but soon the long lines of tanks would make it possible to pump water into the mine.

Cherry had no cemetery. Now the town needed a big one.

The president of the Chicago, Milwaukee & St. Paul Railroad, the biggest customer of the mine, offered to give a cemetery to the stricken community and assume all costs of burying the dead. Experts of the U. S. Geological Survey arrived, studied conditions, and estimated that the fire would be smothered in four or five days. Then the seal could be broken and the grim task of removing the dead could begin in earnest.

Three hundred feet below, George Eddy knew nothing of the futile attempt to enter the mine. But after many hours had passed he realized that he and his men faced a grim ordeal.

Water was already a matter of life or death. Some of the men were openly grumbling. Ine Antoniese, almost delirious, began shouting that he'd rather suffocate than die of thirst.

George Eddy picked eight of the most experienced men, divided them into pairs and set them to exploring every inch of their prison. Hours later one party found a damp spot where there was a minute flow of seepage—a stream no larger than a straw.

Desperate fingers clawed at the rough surface and found five vulnerable spots. When all possible debris had been removed, Eddy led in scratching a shallow groove at the base of the wall. After many minutes it filled with water. There was not enough to get a good swallow and it was thick with coal dust. But parched men eagerly sucked the precious moisture.

After that William Cleland led religious services at intervals. Not a man in the group had a watch and they had long lost all track of time.

Hunger was beginning to pinch. George Eddy decided to save two safety lamps for emergencies. All the rest he divided among the men, who broke them open and ate the wax. Most of them had plug tobacco. It helped as long as it lasted.

They chewed the leather bands from their caps, then tried to gnaw their shoes. William Hines had bad teeth so he gave his shoes to John Lorimer and tore a chunk of bark off a pine shoring. He found it better than he had expected so soon his companions were gnawing at the timbers.

Thomas Bayliss, paymaster, had a dog-eared time book and a lead pencil in his pocket. At the suggestion of their leader he tore pages out of it and passed them around so that men might write notes to their survivors. There were not enough pages to go around.

Joe Pigati had wrapped his lunch in brown paper. Now he salvaged it and wrote his wife a note typical of them all:

"I think my time has come. You know what my property is. We worked for it together, and it is all yours. This is my will and you must keep it. It has been very quiet down here, and I wonder what has become of our comrades. Goodbye."

After that the imprisoned men slept most of the time. Cleland continued to sing and pray but no longer said anything about rescue.

Above ground all hope had been abandoned days ago. At best only the bodies of the dead could be recovered. As early as Sunday experts of the Illinois Mining Commission had said that no man in Cherry Mine could still be alive. Since that was the case it was best to keep the fire capped until it was completely under control. Delay of a few days in reopening it would make no difference.

Late Thursday afternoon the mine was unsealed for the second time. Engineers from the Columbia School of Mines demonstrated use of new oxygen helmets. Tank cars were lined up near the shaft, and fire apparatus was made ready. Led by veteran mine expert R. Y. Williams, Chicago firemen who had never before been in a mine climbed down the shaft. They found flames at the second level, so played water on the smoldering coal for a day and night.

Other volunteers began to hoist bodies to the surface one or two at a time. No building in Cherry was big enough to hold the dead, so bodies were laid in rows in an open field.

Uniformed trained nurses of the Red Cross were on hand in spite of objections by mining company officials. Their presence, said a spokesman, tended to raise false hopes by suggesting that some survivor might be found.

In spite of round-the-clock work by firemen there seemed little hope of getting the blaze under control. It was decided that as many victims as possible should be recovered. Then the mine would be closed indefinitely.

By Saturday afternoon, a full week after the blaze started, a party searching for bodies on the second level thought they heard a dull tapping.

It was George Eddy. He had no thought of rescue, but was pounding on the chamber wall in an attempt to increase the flow of seepage.

Outside in the main tunnel eager hands pulled the barricade aside. As the first light of torches penetrated the chamber, trapped miners shielded their eyes from the glare. Too weak to be demonstrative, those who could walk staggered toward their rescuers.

William Cleland was so grimy and emaciated that he was not recognized by his own brother. Frank, a Frenchman, died on the way to the surface. All the rest of Eddy's band regained their strength after rest and medical treatment.

Three days later, when most of the dead had been recovered, flames again got out of control. Cherry Mine was sealed with a heavy layer of cement and steel, to be reopened at some undetermined time in the future.

Official statistics of the tragedy report only the 259 bodies that were recovered, though all observers agreed that fifty to one hundred and fifty dead were left in the burning mine when it was sealed for the last time.

Because Cherry Mine was one of the newest and most modern in the nation, considered a model of safety in the industry, no sweeping reforms were triggered by the disaster. All testimony indicated that there was no overwhelming instance of carelessness on the part of operators. Many relatively minor factors had combined to produce one of the most costly mining disasters in United States history.

Because George Eddy and his band of twenty miners had lived under conditions considered impossible, the attitude toward rescue activities underwent dramatic change.

"From this day," an official of the U. S. Geological Survey said late that Saturday evening, "we must strike the word 'impossible' from our vocabulary. Men who endured for 171 hours without food or water have shown that we can never again write off a trapped miner as hopeless until he has been found dead."

Officially as well as unofficially, heroism of men who held out days after hope for them had been abandoned proved to be the catalytic agent necessary to spur the nation into a mood of doggedness in rescue attempts, even when logic says that such efforts are useless.

*March 25, 1911*
*New York City*

# 11 Triangle Shirt Waist Fire

Baal-worshipers of ancient Babylon occasionally burned humans on the sacrificial altar. As a result they are sometimes thought of as fiends.

Their achievements were amateurish and trifling. Dollar-worshipers of modern America have done much better. A single pyre once claimed 146 victims. It flared briefly in top floors of the Joseph J. Asch Building, New York City. But the afterglow of the sacrificial fire still lingers in the reforms it produced.

One side of the deadly triangle was made up of a manufacturing system that placed profits above safety. Another side was formed by loose practices in the fire insurance business. The third and final side that served to close the trap was civic pride: Manhattan's stubborn pride in refusing to admit existence of a factory district and taking routine measures to protect workers.

Firemen and police officers had never seen anything like the blaze that flashed through the Triangle Shirt Waist Company on March 25, 1911. For stupidity, greed, and sheer horror it remains unique among U. S. industrial disasters.

69

Forty victims jumped to their deaths. They hit the ground with such rapidity that fire hoses were put out of commission, with such force that gaping holes were torn in cement and steel sidewalk covers.

Five score died in the flames; half of them were charred beyond recognition. Coroner Holtzhauser, hardened to blood and violence, broke into sobs as he saw the first pile of slim, girlish bodies.

In a district like Manhattan, why didn't the fire engines get there?

They did.

Engine Co. #18, led by Foreman Howard Ruch, had a high-pressure hose beside the building before the fire was six minutes old. Company #72 rounded the corner before survivors began to spill from the doomed building. Hook and Ladder Company #20, loaded with extension ladders and nets, was at the site long before police were able to establish a fire line.

From the beginning, however, it was a case of too little too late.

Before the first hose was connected a few girls had jumped. Their blazing clothes made an eerie whistle terminated by a sickening thud. Some had crawled out on cornices. Battalion Chief Worth used his first two lines to cool the building over their heads. Then a gust of wind sucked flames out of windows into the clothes and hair of the trapped girls. Singly for the most part, but sometimes holding hands, they closed their eyes and jumped.

Ladders shot upward with precision and speed. Five girls clinging to an eighth-floor ledge wept as a ladder wobbled toward them. It hesitated, then lurched to a halt two stories short of their perch.

Water. Sure, water would conquer the fire.

Half the high-pressure lines were pressed flat by piles of dead. Though the rest pumped precious liquid into high fire towers, it became a futile stream of spray by the time it stabbed toward the 80-foot level.

There were still the nets. Thank God for the nets!

Company #18 spread the first—brand new and a full fourteen feet long. Three girls dived simultaneously from the ninth floor. They ripped the net to shreds and pulled a dozen firemen inward on top of the victims' bodies.

Company #20 set up the pride and joy of the unit—a twenty-foot Browder net. Bodies rained on it so rapidly that the tube-steel frame buckled and gave way.

Two frenzied policemen yanked a heavy blanket from a horse. They had hardly spread it before a girl plunged. Miraculously, she hit it dead center—and ripped through to crash against the grating of a skylight.

Fire Chief Edward L. Croker had repeatedly told city authorities that he could not fight a blaze above the seventh floor of a building. The first seven floors of the Asch Building, which housed the doomed sweatshop, were virtually undamaged.

But only the Triangle Shirt Waist Company, occupying the top three floors of the building, had remained open that day due to rush business and ordered all employees to make the Jewish Sabbath an ordinary nine-hour work day. As a result seven floors that could be protected with available equipment were empty; three floors beyond reach of fire fighters were crowded with workers.

Survivors had no idea of how the blaze began. Sparks may have flashed from a defective armature on one of the seven big motors used to provide power for sewing machines. Or it may have come as a result of friction in a high-speed shaft. It is possible that some careless worker had dropped a match or cigarette butt into scraps of oily pattern paper.

This much was certain: the fire originated near a cutting table on the eighth floor. A bell had just given the signal for "power off" at 4:45; most machine operators had begun to move toward washrooms. Tables were covered with material for Sunday's work—thick piles of flimsy lawn with tissue paper below each layer of cloth. One pile flared, then another.

Flames darted upward and outward. Long lines of finished shirtwaists hung down the room. These caught and flared. Cotton cords burned through dropping flaming garments into rag bins and on top of worktables piled high with muslin and lace.

Anna Gullo and half a dozen other girls grabbed buckets and dipped water from an open barrel. They soon saw they

71

were getting nowhere and quit. One girl still clutched a fire pail when her broken body was picked up from the sidewalk.

Stairways were only thirty-three inches wide. As was customary in garment factories, one side was locked. The open stair could be approached only through a narrow corridor that was lined with rag bins. This procedure forced departing workers to file out slowly with handbags open so that watchmen could be sure no one was stealing scraps.

Now the passageway proved a deathtrap. Scraps had piled up for ten weeks. Flames from rag bins generated so much gas that eighth-floor windows blew out about the time the unlocked stairway was completely cut off by flames.

There were four elevators—two for passengers and two for freight. On the Washington Street side of the building Giuseppe Zito ran his car until he fainted. Locked cars on the Greene Street side were opened and used for four or five round trips to the street level.

Workers on the doomed eighth floor had just one other avenue of escape—a single narrow fire escape. Leo Todor climbed all the way to the bottom, falling several times as he squeezed past cast-iron shutters that blocked some landings.

For most, the fire escape proved another grim joke. Less than twenty who tried this route survived. Too flimsy to stand either the heat or the weight thrown upon it, the iron ladder warped and then gave way. Many who hung on it fell or were forced to jump.

Heat from the ninth floor was so intense that it warped sheet-iron shutters on another building twenty feet away.

By this time only the strongest were still clinging to cornices and window ledges. Most girls had a superstitious fear of not being identified, so preferred to be smashed rather than burned.

Rosie Yusum testified that when a girl's skirt caught fire, she would say a prayer, knot a rag about her eyes, and step out into space.

It was all over by 5:15. Floors and partitions continued to smolder, but the intense flames had lasted only eighteen minutes.

By this time twenty-five police patrol wagons were at the scene. Fire lines alone required 150 men. Deputy Commissioner Driscoll used others to begin removing bodies from the sidewalk.

At first he estimated about forty dead. Then firemen found gruesome piles in elevator shafts and ordered the morgue to prepare seventy-five coffins. At 7:00 floors had cooled sufficiently to enter the ninth floor; white-lipped, Driscoll looked about only an instant before sending an order to double the number of coffins.

Profiting from experience gained after the burning of the *General Slocum* less than a decade earlier, firemen tagged bodies where they were found. Transferred into open coffins victims soon overflowed the morgue, so auxiliary lines were established on an adjoining dock. By 11:30 there were 136 bodies. Thirteen were known to be men. All the rest were women or beyond identification.

Back of the tragedy were social and economic forces that made it not merely possible, but inevitable.

Prominent among these was greed of those who owned and operated garment industries. Here management had launched a last desperate offensive against labor unions.

It was at Triangle that the great shirtwaist strike of 1910 had started. It spread until 40,000 workers were out. They pawned furniture to buy food, braved hostile police, and won contracts with many shops. Triangle refused to sign and eventually broke the strike.

Max Blanck and Isaac Harris, owners, used two devices to keep wages down. They hired girls of thirteen and fourteen as messengers. After paying them $4.50 a week for a few months, they promoted the messengers to sewing on buttons at $6.00 a week. By the time a girl reached sixteen she usually picked up enough skill to take over a machine for a $3 raise.

To supplement this source of labor, owners recruited newly arrived immigrants. Most of them were skilled at finger work and quickly became expert runners, trimmers, and slopers. Hired at $6 a week, they were given occasional raises until they reached a top of about $12. Piece rates spurred slow workers to develop speed; as soon as they did, they were transferred to straight wages. By working thirteen hours a day seven days a week, a few fast girls earned as much as $18 a week.

Use of immigrants created many special problems after the fire. In thirty-seven cases, dead girls left dependent relatives

73

abroad—in Russia, Austria, Hungary, Romania, Palestine, Ireland, and Italy.

Insurance practices stacked more cards against workers. Agents and brokers collected their commissions on a percentage basis. This meant that their cuts rose with rates. Instead of aiming at safety conditions that would reduce risks and rates, pressure groups pushed for bigger premiums whenever losses provided an excuse.

It would not have required a trouble-shooter to identify Harris and Blanck as bad risks. Their Triangle shops had had four blazes in the decade which preceded the holocaust of 1911; Diamond Waist Company, which they also operated, had fires in 1906, 1909, and 1910.

Harris and Blanck were headed for the financial rocks; their creditors had a provisional meeting on the morning of the disaster. Triangle's insurance was increased $35,000 during 1910— yet the premium on a $75,000 policy that was renewed in January, 1911, remained unpaid until days after the fire.

Factory managers and insurance agents drew two sides of an ominous triangle; real estate operators whose practices were fostered by civic pride closed the figure and made tragedy inevitable.

So far as official records were concerned, downtown New York had no factory building. But in 1911 the city held an estimated 30,000 factories scattered through 12,000 buildings.

Most were housed in what real estate promoters called "loft buildings." These structures came into vogue about 1895 and provided low-rent space. In the decade that prepared the way for the Triangle fire 790 lofts were thrown up in Greater New York. Among them was the Asch Building at 23 Washington Place.

Fire codes limited the height of apartment houses and required theaters to install sprinkler systems. Neither condition applied to lofts.

Strong appeals for more and bigger equipment with which to fight fires were turned down because new taxes would be involved.

During the trial for manslaughter, the case against Harris and Blanck turned on the question of whether or not they personally ordered the ninth floor stairway to be locked. Jurors freed them on the third ballot and met a storm of public protest. Gradually, however, indignation was turned into constructive channels. Editorials laid the blame on society as well as operators of the Triangle Co.

No charges were preferred against city or state building inspectors, license agencies, insurance brokers, or builders. But before the year ended New York State issued a 3,000-page report on *Corrupt Practices in Insurance Companies Other than Life*.

Edward Croker had won an international reputation during twelve years as Chief of the New York Fire Department. Now he turned in his badge in order to lead a crusade for safety.

"Fire-fighting has gone about as far as it can for the present," he said. "We've come to the place where we've got to keep fires from starting."

Legislators throughout the nation examined and revised fire codes. New York led the way with the Sullivan-Hoey Fire Prevention Law of October, 1911. This gave a single Fire Commission the powers formerly divided among six agencies. Owners of factory buildings were required to install automatic sprinkler systems, and a Division of Fire Prevention was launched.

America has had disasters in which loss of life was much greater, but few were followed by more significant reforms.

December 6, 1917
Halifax, Nova Scotia

# 12 Explosion in Halifax Harbor

During World War I, many ships that moved men and material across the Atlantic made Halifax, Nova Scotia, a major stopping place. The harbor was one of the biggest and safest in the entire North Atlantic.

Each night huge nets were swung across the harbor to prevent German U-boats from entering. Big batteries of artillery guarded the coast for miles on each side of the city. Consequently both citizens of the shipping center and seamen who visited it felt removed from the terrors of war. Even the sight of heavily loaded munitions vessels and piles of explosives on the docks did not dispel this mood of relative complacency.

On the morning of December 6, 1917, everything was routine until approximately 8:40. During the following minutes blunders and errors set off chain reactions whose end result was explosion of more than eight million tons of TNT—dwarfing every other accidental explosion in recorded history.

Robert L. Burns, who later spent many years as a worker for the Pennsylvania Railroad and retired in Claymont, Delaware, had vivid memories of the fateful day after fifty-five years.

"I was a crew member of the U.S.S. *Von Steuben*," he said. "We were on our way home from France, ran short of coal and turned in to Halifax in order to get a supply.

"Our ship was just entering the harbor when the explosion took place. We didn't know the cause, but realized that every able-bodied man would be needed in rescue work. So we went into the harbor, anchored, and all hands aboard—nine hundred of us—did what we could to help victims of the disaster.

"While our vessel was anchored inside the breakwater the wind picked up and soon reached gale speed. Inside the breakwater a small Great Lakes steamer, the *North Wind*, began dragging her anchor and smashed into our ship. We had enough steam to start our engines and we could hold our own against the storm, so no one on our ship was killed. If we had arrived an hour earlier, most or all of us would have gone sky-high."

It was routine for all vessels entering the harbor to be guided through the narrows by experienced local pilots. Frank Mackie, a skilled Canadian, was in charge of the motor launch to which the French munitions vessel *Mont Blanc* was assigned.

Mackie took care of usual formalities, then about 8:40 signaled for the heavily loaded vessel to ease her way toward docks already crowded with naval personnel of several nations plus men loading and unloading big ships.

So far there was no hint of anything wrong.

The sun was shining, there was only a hint of a breeze, and fog that had been noticed at dawn had already disappeared. It should have been only a matter of minutes before the *Mont Blanc* would be resting safely at anchor.

As the big French vessel moved slowly around a bend in the channel, however, her pilot was jarred out of his casual mood. Dead ahead of him another ship he could not for the moment identify was bearing straight toward the *Mont Blanc* and her cargo of explosives.

Following standard procedures familiar to seamen of the entire western world, the outgoing vessel blew a short, last blast with her whistle. This was a signal that she would pass to the starboad of the incoming ship.

Pilot Frank Mackie signaled and the *Mont Blanc* altered her course a bit to comply with his orders. But something went

77

wrong; the two ships were continuing on a collision course. About the time the alarm system of the French ship burst into action, Mackie identified the outgoing vessel as the Belgian steamer *Imo*. Designed for the commercial trade she had been pressed into wartime service with few alterations in structure. Today she was heavily loaded and sitting low in the water. Grain was so desperately needed in her homeland that every possible ton of wheat had been poured into the *Imo*.

Her heavy load made the Belgian vessel sluggish. In spite of her signal, she was headed directly toward the incoming munitions ship.

On the bridge of the *Mont Blanc* the helmsman did his best. But by spinning his wheel he succeeded only in maneuvering his vessel into such a position that her hull—the most vulnerable part of the ship—was directly in front of the *Imo's* sharp prow.

Robert Burns said that survivors swore the accident was a freak; as they spun apart after a jarring collision, the *Imo* was seen to be practically unhurt—while the hull of the munitions ship was ripped open all the way to the water line. Even in calm seas she would soon be shipping more water than her pumps could handle.

That matter proved academic; pumps never had a chance to go into action. Barrels of fuel stored in the forward section of the *Mont Blanc* were ruptured by the crash. Fire came from somewhere. Perhaps it was generated by the impact of steel upon steel. Or a few gallons of benzol may have squirted as far as a charcoal fire that French crew members customarily kept going in the forecastle.

Weeks of legal inquiry never settled the question of how the fire got started.

To crewmen on that frosty December day the only thing that mattered was getting off the *Mont Blanc* before she went up in smoke. So they made only a brief and perfunctory attempt to put out the fire. Already spreading rapidly, it promised to engulf the entire vessel in a matter of minutes.

Frightened seamen soon won their captain's permission to abandon ship. They got into small boats, rowed to the dock area, and began shouting warnings: "Pou-dar! Pou-dar!"

Most persons who heard them didn't understand what they were saying. A few who did turned and raced after the fleeing sailors.

H.M.S. *Highflyer*, a British cruiser, was anchored near the point of impact between the colliding vessels. Officers knew the *Mont Blanc* to be a munitions carrier, so ordered a boat into the water, and sent men to try to save the blazing ship.

Most of the twenty-three British were aboard the *Mont Blanc* when the munitions carrier exploded. The ship burst and slowly fell apart. Smoke and flames were shot high into the sky. Fragments of the *Mont Blanc* pelted down upon the central waterfront of Halifax. One half-ton segment of the ship's anchor was hurled three miles.

So great was the blast that plates danced about breakfast tables on Prince Edward Island, 125 miles away.

Water rushed outward from the area where the *Mont Blanc* had been, then roared back in a tidal wave so fearful that it ripped big ships from their moorings and tossed them, helpless, on the shore.

Richmond, a community on the southern shores of Halifax Narrows, was so situated that pressure waves sweeping through a trough between hills hit with the speed and power of a hurricane.

In Richmond School teachers thought it was an earthquake. They shouted for children to leave the quivering buildings; before they could get out of their seats, 197 were killed.

Vincent Coleman, telegraph operator at the Richmond station, had seen the collision from the distance. He tapped out a last message: "MUNITIONS SHIP ON FIRE MAKING FOR PIER 8 GOODBYE." Clean-up crews who dug through debris the next day found Coleman's body with his finger close to the telegraph key.

In Halifax itself the explosion came so suddenly that hardly anyone realized what had caused it. There were shouts of "Air raid!" in spite of the fact that no German aircraft had approached within hundreds of miles. Many considered the upheaval to be due to an earthquake. Some knelt in the streets and prayed, sure that Judgment Day had come.

Meanwhile fire threatened those portions of the waterfront

that had not already been flattened. It crept slowly toward ammunition dumps in which many more thousands of tons of explosives were stored. At great risk, an entire naval battery fought the flames and got unexpected aid when a surging tide flooded the area with sea water and doused the fire.

Rescue workers later found that two and one half square miles of the city had been destroyed. Frenzied dogs, cats, horses, goats, and cattle dashed through the streets while 5,000 survivors began gathering in the city's commons.

"That's the situation we found when our vessel reached what we had expected to find a haven and a place to relax a few hours," Robert Burns said. "That day, authorities were already saying they would never know exactly how many casualties were claimed by the explosion. Later the official count of dead stopped at about 1500. That did not include hundreds listed as 'missing,' or another 20,000 who were hurt."

Investigating the most fearful accident that took place during World War I, authorities were reluctant to assign blame. Eventually a court of inquiry ruled that the explosion had been caused by "negligence upon the part of captain and crew of the steamer *Imo*." Another court placed the guilt upon men of the *Mont Blanc*. Eventually the highest tribunal of England, the Privy Council, found both groups of seamen equally at fault.

A few officers were relieved of their posts. Some enlisted men were reprimanded. Then the case was closed.

Hoping to wipe out the past, owners of the *Imo* refurbished the damaged ship and gave her a new name. Precisely five years after she hit the *Mont Blanc*, on December 6, 1921, the Belgian vessel hit a hidden reef in the Falkland Islands and sank.

Halifax suffered more damage and a greater number of casualties than some cities involved in hand-to-hand combat between Allied troops and iron-helmeted subjects of the German kaiser. But no sweeping reforms in handling of explosives followed. There were no changes in time-hallowed rituals governing movements of ships in crowded harbors.

More than anything else the Halifax disaster served to underscore the fact that when war is raging, a catastrophe far from combat zones receives relatively little attention.

*July 9, 1918*
*Nashville, Tennessee*

# 13 America's Worst Railroad Wreck

At least 101 persons died in a head-on collision of two fast
trains on July 9, 1918. Believed due to human error that could
have been avoided, the death toll exceeded that of any other
United States train wreck. Yet news of it never was widely
circulated, and even in cities most directly affected, the event
was dropped from the front pages within seventy-two hours.

About 7:15 A.M. on Tuesday—the second full day of work
after a long Fourth of July holiday and celebration—Nashville, Chattanooga, and St. Louis train #4 approached the signal
tower in newly completed shops about five miles west of Tennessee's capital city.

That evening the *Nashville Banner* ran banner headlines and
devoted five columns of the front page to the disaster. But
even the carnage near the city could not crowd off the front
page a two-column account of French military advances along
a two-and-one-half-mile front near Anthueil and astride the
Compeigne Road. The *Nashville Tennessean* headlines on
Wednesday morning reported a death toll of 121 (later revised

downward) at the edge of the city. But the front page also carried an account of French victories under General Foch on the Lys front.

Strangely, the conflict in Europe that gripped national attention so firmly that America's worst rail disaster is virtually unknown was a precipitating factor in creating a climate leading to that disaster.

Survivors were emphatic in stressing the fact that David C. Kennedy, engineer of the doomed westbound train, blew for his signal "in the customary manner." Kennedy's train was about to leave a section of double track. Schedules called for the eastbound Memphis express to pass his train on that section. Since it hadn't, the express was obviously running late. This created a dilemma.

If the Memphis express was still twenty to thirty minutes away, Kennedy could proceed safely. But if it was less than twenty minutes away he'd have to wait. Ahead of him loomed a ten-mile stretch of single track.

So the engineer's whistle constituted a question in railroad code: "What's the situation? Shall I stop and wait, or go ahead?"

Witnesses said that Kennedy's whistle got a clear board—shorthand for "O.K. to proceed; track clear." But testimony in the official hearing indicated that before train #4 had passed through the shop area, the red board dropped in a desperate but futile attempt to signal: "Stop!"

The local train from Nashville, the locomotive and cars guided by Kennedy, had slowed to about ten miles per hour as the signal tower was approached. Puffing heavily in order to pull up the long, curving slope known as Dutchman's Grade, the engine was out of sight of the signal board when orders were reversed.

From the other direction passenger train #1 from Memphis and St. Louis had the advantage of gravity. So the crack express was roaring down Dutchman's Grade at more than sixty miles an hour in an attempt to make up lost time.

Engines collided; and the two locomotives reared and fell beside the track.

Coaches of the westbound local train were lightly built. Those of the express were heavy-duty ones designed for long runs at high speed. With locomotives out of the way big coaches of the express train hit those of the local so hard that they telescoped almost instantly.

The two engines, three baggage cars, and six passenger cars were demolished. Hot coals spewed from engine boilers started a fire that quickly got out of control.

Practically all riders on the local train were workers at the DuPont powder plant on the outskirts of Nashville. Haste of the express was partly due to the fact that it brought another two hundred men coming to aid the war effort by offering their services at the same plant.

Both engineers, both firemen, and a baggage master were killed on impact. It was hours before anyone had firm information about the number of passengers killed and injured.

More than forty men were pinned beneath a single crumpled car. Some died quickly; others cried for help. A few who believed their plight to be hopeless implored police officers to shoot them.

Huge jacks and other heavy equipment stood in railroad yards only a few miles away. By the time rescue workers managed to lift the crushed car from men upon whom it lay, only one was still alive.

Willie Tillman, foreman of a crew of forty-five men coming in from Little Rock, somehow emerged from the wreck without a scratch. Though he had only one arm, Tillman managed to get his window down in the seconds that revealed an impending crash. He jumped out unhurt, did his best to pull survivors from wreckage, then spent the next three days searching Nashville morgues for the fifteen men of his crew who died.

W. M. Winstead, one of several youthful soldiers killed, carried an unmailed letter in his pocket.

"War is tough," he had written his parents, "but things aren't always easy in civilian life. I'm going to be all right. When you hear from me next, I'll be in France."

Nashville resident Leland Moore was more fortunate. He escaped, he said afterward, because he waited to hear a funny story that a friend was telling. Other passengers had urged him to go with them to the smoker, from which no one emerged without serious injury.

"The scene immediately following the collision is indescribable," a veteran reporter wrote. "Those escaping unhurt or with lesser injuries fled from the spot in a veritable panic. The cornfield on both sides of the track was trampled by many feet, and littered with fragments of iron and wood hurled from the demolished cars. The dead lay here and there, grotesquely sprawling where they fell. The dying moaned appeals for aid or, speechless, rolled their heads from side to side and writhed in agony."

Crowds of curious, never counted but estimated to number "at least eight thousand," flocked to the scene of the catastrophe.

Long before noon city hospitals were crowded with an estimated 140 injured, while the morgue began to overflow within an hour after the first bodies were recovered from the wreckage.

An unidentified workman bought flags and insisted on the privilege of arranging one about the body of each dead soldier.

Identification was often difficult and frequently impossible. In the nightmare moments of the wreck, a boiler from an engine toppled against a crushed passenger car and seared many victims beyond recognition.

As rapidly as out-of-town victims could be identified, their bodies were boxed for shipment. At the height of the activity thirty-eight coffins, stacked like cordwood, stood outside a single funeral parlor. Unidentified and unclaimed bodies were consigned to representatives of the U. S. government.

This procedure stemmed from the fact that the N. C. & St. L., like all U. S. railroads, was then under government operation as a wartime measure. A major factor motivating Congress to order take-over of the nation's railroads was "imperative necessity for efficient and safe operation in this time of national emergency."

Because of the strange position in which railroads found themselves, legal consequences of the crash on Dutchman's Grade were without precedent.

President Peyton of the N. C. & St. L. arrived at the scene while bodies were still being taken away. He expressed "deep personal sorrow," and simultaneously issued a statement indicating that the railroad had no legal liability since it was being operated by the government.

Formal hearings began on Saturday, July 13.

Rumor had it that engineer Kennedy had died with a timetable in his hand—an indication that he recognized the danger but was trying to beat the eastbound train through the section of single track in order to reach a switch at Harding Junction.

Though this evidence was not admitted, the panel of experts and legal advisers ruled that the wreck occurred because crew members of train #4 "failed to see signals, or disregarded them."

C. H. Markham, federally appointed regional director of the railroads, issued a statement even before formal hearings began. "It will be the policy of the Government to discourage litigation and to deal directly with injured persons to the end that claimants may receive the broadest benefits without expense of litigation," he said.

What this actually meant, as events showed, was that the government would pay out as little as possible and do everything in its power to discourage claimants.

Many cases were settled "by negotiation" for a few hundred dollars each. In the seventeen cases where victims were never legally identified, survivors received no recompense at all. A few families who hired lawyers and threatened suit against the government settled out of court for sums ranging as high as $5,000.

Because the nation's attention was gripped by events in Europe, the crash of two trains attracted only a ripple of interest. Some major newspapers ignored the disaster completely. Others carried short stories on inside pages. A few ran page one stories on the day after the disaster, then promptly dropped coverage.

War—the same war that had prompted government takeover of the railroads in the name of safety and efficiency—made the wreck seem unimportant.

Newsmen considered it vital to run big headlines about the triumph of a president's son: "LT. QUENTIN ROOSEVELT BRINGS DOWN HIS FIRST GERMAN PLANE." It was important to inform readers that "FRENCH SMASH FOR-

WARD A MILE" and reassure them that "NO ARMY WILL BE SENT TO RUSSIA."

Nationally it didn't seem significant that 101 persons, most of them black males who were already on the payroll of a defense plant or were reporting for work, died because members of a train crew wanted to gain a few minutes' time.

Within transportation circles, however, the accident served to spur progress in adoption of automatic signaling devices. Hand-operated signals, hallowed by having been in use since the infancy of railroading, gave way to faster and more accurate ways of communicating with trainmen. To an extent unequaled in United States history, the obscure and all-but-forgotten crash near Nashville served to make rail travel safer than ever before.

May 17, 1923
Kershaw County, South Carolina

# 14 Fiery Death at Beulah School

Thursday was to have been a gala day in the history of Beulah community. In Kershaw County, South Carolina, it was customary to have a public entertainment in connection with the close of the school year. "School closing" in 1923 turned into a tragic disaster in the rural school.

Three teachers were responsible for the elementary education of eighty-six children who lived in the district. They worked and studied in a two-story frame building that was erected in 1909 and named in honor of President Grover Cleveland.

Cleveland School was built better than many in rural districts—but had no fire escapes. They weren't considered necessary. In the event of a blaze a crowd could scurry down the big stairway in a matter of minutes. At worst it would be simple to jump from an upstairs window, not quite twenty feet above the ground.

On the evening closing exercises were to be held, a capacity crowd had gathered by 7:30. Teachers and pupils had practiced for weeks on a three-act play, *Miss Topsy Turvy*. Everyone

87

knew everyone else, and there was hearty good fellowship as the crowd moved up the stairway and into the second-floor auditorium.

A few men stood about outside smoking, but for the most part whole families entered and sat together. Grandparents shared some of the excitement of tots too small to go to school and intent upon missing nothing.

As the hall filled, the Rev. J. J. Johnson, pastor of nearby Camden Baptist Church, took a seat on the front row. He was scheduled to make an address after the play and graduation exercises.

By the time houselights were extinguished, fully one hundred fifty persons were in the building. Mothers and fathers whispered to children, warning them of dire consequences if they were not silent. A chuckle rippled through the audience as a chubby eight-year-old minced to the center of the stage, forgot his opening lines, and turned toward the prompter for assistance.

Conversation buzzed through the house in the brief intermission after Act I. Proud parents beamed their thanks as neighbors congratulated them on the way their Tommy or their Nell seemed "a born actor." A few children ventured to ask permission to get a drink of water, but most were yanked back into their seats.

Act II was a huge success. Hearty applause followed the dropping of the curtain, and teachers sat back with sighs of relief that everything was going well.

Backstage someone turned up the wick of a kerosine lamp as the scenes were being shifted for Act III. The increased heat melted the solder in the bracket from which the lamp hung. Within minutes it crashed to the floor. Little tongues of flame raced along the surface of the kerosine as it spread.

There was no confusion or excitement. The lamp had held less than a pint of oil.

One of the parents helping to change the scenes tried to stamp out the flames. Another who had gone to his assistance grabbed a bundle of cloth and attempted to smother the fire. The flimsy cheesecloth used by the amateur firefighter didn't extinguish the flames. Instead it, too, caught and began to blaze furiously.

By now some in the audience knew that there was trouble backstage. A woman screamed: "Fire! Fire!" There was an instant of stunned silence, then the mass of people packed in the darkened auditorium rose and stampeded for the stairway.

A few were outside the building within thirty seconds. As yet the glare of the blaze was not visible. Then a sleepy child who was stumbling down the stairway lost her footing and fell.

Her father stooped to pick her up, but the mob behind pushed him over. In an instant others tripped over him and the stairway became hopelessly jammed. Behind, the fear-maddened throng threw all their weight against the living barricade and packed it into a human logjam from which legs, heads, and arms protruded crazily.

While this was happening, the flames were spreading rapidly. The fat, dry pine boards burned readily and produced intense heat.

The Baptist minister had escaped in spite of the disadvantage of being seated near the front of the auditorium. Holding his two small daughters in his arms and his son by the hand he had raced for the exit. Near the stair the boy's hand was torn from him and the child was swallowed up in the crowd.

After leading his girls to safety the minister turned back to hunt for his boy. The stairway had become jammed in the few seconds that he was outside the building. Finally he found his son, only inches from the door, trapped beneath a mass of bodies.

Reaching under, Johnson patted his head.

"That's you, Daddy!" exclaimed the youngster.

"Yes, I've come to get you out."

"No, Daddy," the child said feebly, "you can't do it."

As the minister knelt with his hand on the boy's head, his son died—life literally crushed out of him.

Upstairs a few ceased pushing against the mass on the stair and hunted other means of escape. A middle-aged farmer climbed out a window and down to the roof which sheltered the doorway of the building. He jumped sixteen feet to the ground and landed without injury.

With the help of two boys he raised a flagpole against the side of the house, then stood by and caught those who slid down. About twenty women and children careened down the pole; not one was hurt.

At this point, perhaps six minutes after the lamp had fallen, fire gripped only the front one-third of the auditorium.

A youngster home from college kicked out a window and yelled to those below to spread automobile cushions on the ground. They did, and he passed a score of persons to safety, with cushions breaking the force of their fall.

A few others jumped from other windows. Stoney Campbell, one of the last to leave the doomed building, had brought his wife and daughter to the exercises. Early in the melee the girl was separated from her parents. When his wife hesitated to jump, Campbell threw her out the window and then leaped after her. He was momentarily dazed, then recovered and began searching for his daughter.

He soon found her in the front part of the pile in the stairway. Only the lower half of her body was caught. Campbell tried to pull her out but could not. Four men turned to help him; while flames drew nearer, they pulled like madmen. Both arms of the girl snapped from the shoulder sockets but her body did not budge.

Then the roof began to fall upon the trapped mass. Wesley Hendrix, prominent landowner, was only a yard from the door. His clothing and hair were on fire but he was smiling. Campbell tried to get him out but Hendrix shook his head. "I'm a man," he said, "and I'll die like a man."

Other would-be rescuers perished because they tried to help friends. The outer edge of the heap was in constant movement; a few were pulled out, and others were drawn into the mass. Jess Pearce, hunting for his wife, discovered a neighbor held only by one leg. He managed to pull him free, but in the process was himself shoved into the jam. Friends broke his arm trying to yank him out, but failed.

Some of those packed into the stairway were unconscious or dead. But most of them, whether in the barricade itself or waiting in the auditorium above, were fully conscious. As the wind threw flames into the mass of people, shrieks of the dying rose above the roar of the blaze. Not even the odor of burning pine could disguise the stench of human flesh, roasted and seared while still alive.

A few survivors were overcome by nausea and retched violently. Most of them stood by wringing their hands and crying as they watched the flames bite deeper and deeper into the structure. Soon a group of blazing timbers gave way and the entire building fell in upon the trapped mass.

Next morning very little debris was to be found at the scene of the disaster. A picnic had been planned for the forenoon and many chickens had been fried in preparation for it. A few children who lived on outer edges of the school district did not know of the tragedy. They walked gaily to the school with their lunch baskets only to be greeted by a few twisted bits of tin, smoking ashes, and the charred remains of seventy-seven friends and relatives.

Identification of the dead was seen to be a hopeless task from the beginning. Here and there a piece of jewelry, a belt buckle, a charred scrap of clothing gave a clue.

By Saturday only thirteen of the dead had been tentatively identified. A great pile of human scraps remained. Few bodies were whole. Most of the torsos were left in some cases, but in others the only relic was a leg, an arm, or a charred bone.

A huge grave was dug, forty feet long and twelve feet wide. The pitiful bits of bodies were wrapped in sheeting and placed in a single wooden box. Undertakers estimated that it contained all that was left of sixty-four persons.

Unlike most fires the Cleveland School holocaust was a total disaster for the community. Few families were untouched; some were wiped out. More than one-third of the pupils in the school perished. Not a member of the fourth grade was left alive. Thompson Davis, barely seventeen years old, lost his father, mother, and two sisters. He was left to manage the farm and be both father and mother to a baby of nine months plus girls aged two, five, and six.

Seeking to erase all signs of the disaster survivors dug a big pit and buried the ashes of the building. Two big oaks, twisted and bent by the heat of the inferno, were cut down and destroyed. The ground was leveled and grass was planted.

Today the only tangible reminder of the tragedy is a bronze

plaque in the nearby church. But after half a century the scars still disfigure Beulah community. Even the coming of new generations, untroubled by personal memories of the dreadful night, has not been sufficient to dispel the atmosphere of tragedy that marks the district.

All observers agree that the calamity shouldn't have taken place. But survivors point out that it could be reenacted any day in any community that fails to heed two warnings trumpeted by the Cleveland School fire.

The night of hell at the crossroads school emphasizes the fact that no public building is too small to be a deathtrap. There have been numerous American blazes in which loss of life was greater than in Cleveland School, but few if any in which the number of casualties has been so great in comparison with the material loss.

Seventy-seven perished in a building valued at $3,000. It was not conspicuously bad. Had anyone suggested that it constituted a firetrap, taxpayers would have howled in derision. For the structure was no worse than thousands of lodge halls, Sunday school buildings, and rural schools that still dot the nation.

Strike size and value of building from the list of factors central to a community disaster, survivors of the Cleveland School fire urged all who would listen. But never stop stressing the danger of panic.

Had the audience remained calm and orderly, the entire crowd could have filed down the stairway before flames approached the rear of the auditorium. Even after the barricade was formed, many who died above could have jumped from windows.

"Terror makes persons blind," Pastor Johnson said at a simple ceremony held near the mass grave. "Regardless of the nature of the danger, whenever a group of persons face threats to their safety the greatest single threat is panic. That lesson needs to be learned and relearned, over and over, in rural settlements as well as in urban centers."

*March 18, 1925*
*Five Central States*

# 15 The Great Tornado of 1925

Devastation from windstorms, according to the U. S. Weather Bureau, "is an erratic, unpredictable and inescapable condition of life in the midwest."

Growing knowledge has yielded some understanding of tornadoes. They are known to originate when huge masses of hot air from the tropics clash with other masses of air from the north.

They are most frequent in spring, because this is the time when earth's rotation about the sun, coupled with effects of spinning on an axis tipped away from the vertical, causes rapid changes in temperature.

With the coming of spring in temperate zones clashes between air masses are inevitable and spinning movements are inescapable. Most are short-lived and local in their impact. For each one that causes property damage, there are dozens that pass unheeded; for each that results in death, there are hundreds that fail to deliver a lethal punch.

Prof. Henry J. Cox, U. S. Weather Bureau forecaster in Chicago, was following routine procedures of the era when on March 18, 1925, he indicated that "a typical Middle-West spring-time storm" was brewing.

Middlewestern, it certainly was. Typical in behavior perhaps, but not in effects.

A mass of hot air over the Gulf of Lower California clashed with a cold front moving down from Canada. Enormous quantities of energy—estimated to be many times as great as the energy involved in the bombing of Hiroshima—were released. Rotation of the earth caused eddies of air at the edge of the system to begin spinning.

The storm passed over Colorado without doing more than minor and local damage.

A few hours later it dipped briefly into Arkansas, but still showed no signs of becoming a killer. Then, said meteorologists, "nature took the path of least resistance—air rushed into the Ohio Valley."

Dipping downward before it actually reached this natural channel, wind brought death and destruction to Missouri. With the full fury of the storm now unleashed more than half a continent away from the area where it originated, it left a path of devastation across Illinois.

Some of its energy was now dissipated. But it practically leveled towns in southwestern Indiana, then made a few lethal swipes at nearby Kentucky and Tennessee.

With its destructive force spent, the storm spawned in semitropical zones rushed off in the direction of Iceland in the form of a high wind without accompanying twisters.

Official figures list the death toll at 680; property damage ran into many millions.

Southern Illinois, hardest hit, was described by combat veterans as "looking like a World War I battlefield." Murphysboro, West Frankfort, and De Soto accounted for more than 400 victims.

Princeton, Indiana, with a death toll of only twenty but a pattern of destruction few Americans had seen, became a mecca for the curious.

Five days after the twister, on March 23, an estimated 100,000 persons from Chicago, St. Louis, Louisville, Indianapolis, and points between poured into the stricken Indiana town. Nearby Griffin, where fifty died, was kept under strict martial law and closed to sightseers.

"Bent upon seeing effects of the greatest catastrophe ever visited upon this region," an Evansville, Indiana, paper reported, "the curious taxed the strength of re-enforced military lines."

Cars passed through the Baldwin Heights area of Princeton, worst hit section of the town, at a rate of twenty-five per minute. Many urban families had brought picnic lunches, hoping to spread them in the area between Princeton and Owensville.

National guardsmen stood on duty clad in steel helmets and holding rifles with fixed bayonets, but permitted thousands to spread their lunches in a region whose shattered farm buildings gave it a resemblance to battlefields of France. When guardsmen would permit them to do so, sightseers ate fried chicken and drank lukewarm lemonade or beer in the lee of fallen tree trunks and collapsed buildings.

For those who saw the storm hit and who survived its fury, there were no picnics.

Memorial services for more than 600 dead in stricken sections of five states were held on March 22, the first Sunday after the elements laid waste a five-hundred mile stretch of territory.

Town leaders of Murphysboro, Illinois, debated alternatives and solemnly concluded that it would be best to hold a single memorial service for the 189 then known to be dead. In nearby West Frankfort, Illinois, the death toll reached 122 before being revised downward and then back upward.

Everywhere hospitals had overflowed and emergency clinics had been established in public buildings. More than 2,900 persons who lived through the hours of terror were treated for serious injuries.

Some small towns were virtually wiped off the map. Whole blocks of larger places were leveled, and fire added to horrors of the wind.

De Soto, Illinois, a hamlet of 500 persons, looked as though it had been chosen as a target for a raid by heavy bombers. Murphysboro lost nearly three square miles of its business and residential sections.

Red Cross officials issued "a crying call" for tents to aid stricken families. Some occupied temporary housing for days before they could be relocated.

Supplies of antitetanus serum ran low in major cities near the devastated area then were exhausted. Officials of an Indianapolis drug manufacturing firm secured 750 tubes, last of the available supply in that city, and sent them to Carbondale and Murphysboro, Illinois. Delivery was by air—a feat still comparatively unusual and spectacular.

A reporter who flew over the ruins of West Frankfort, Illinois, dictated a description from the air.

"On the day after the winds hit, as far as the eye could see at dawn there stretched a huge irregular mass of debris. Haggard rescue workers and survivors of storm-victims paused only briefly to gaze at a sunrise barren of the hope of a new day.

"Indiscriminately mingled were houses, wires, poles, and automobiles. Confusion reigned supreme—confusion, grief, and death.

"From the field north of the famed Orient Mine blackened figures could be seen probing the ruins of their homes dressed just as they were when called from the depths of the earth to find families annihilated."

Griffin, Indiana, was struck precisely at 4:10 P.M. Though the blast lasted less than ten minutes, shattered ruins of four houses were all that remained of the town's two hundred buildings.

Incredibly no person among the hundreds who had witnessed the storm reported having seen a clearly defined tornado funnel. Even had funnels been sighted, there was no effective warning system in operation.

U. S. government officials began struggling with the problem of warning citizens about tornadoes before the Civil War. There was no concerted effort, however, until the 1870's. During that decade the U. S. Army Signal Corps launched the practice of issuing warnings or "probabilities." They did so over the objections of numerous national leaders who feared that any attempt to issue forecasts would do more harm than good by engendering panic.

Subsequently taken over by the U. S. Weather Bureau, the job of issuing warnings now involves use of radar, computers, radio, and TV. Had today's system of "weather alerts" that often precede tornado warnings been in operation in 1925, many of the storm's victims would still be living.

Savage fury of the 1925 disaster greatly accelerated progress toward nationwide weather alerts delivered at high speed. Because of such alerts no subsequent storm of its type has claimed so many victims as that which struck on March 18 and was momentarily dismissed as "just another typical midwestern blow."

*March 13, 1928*
*Santa Clara Valley, California*

# 16 Collapse
# of the St. Francis Dam

Until 1928 no major dam erected with care and employing "mass concrete" had ever failed. There is always a first. This one came just after midnight on March 13th.

St. Francis Dam was built to guarantee the city of Los Angeles an emergency water supply that would last for ninety days. But when the structure yielded to pressure behind it, the whole thing gave way in a matter of minutes.

Twelve billion gallons of water roared through lush Santa Clara Valley where nearly everyone was asleep.

Summarizing their impressions after the ghastly cleanup, Red Cross nurses stressed the fact that there were few nonfatal injuries. When the soft feet of the mighty dam buckled under their load, persons in the path of galloping water had two alternatives: escape or perish. So most who did not die got out with whole skins.

An estimated seven hundred persons didn't make it. In most cases the choice was made by Fate, whose capricious dealings with men, women, and children swept many to instant death but left alive a few whom logic would have included in the list of the doomed.

Californians outside Los Angeles had generally objected to construction of the dam.

Ranchers who resented the fact that aqueducts took water past their thirsty land had dynamited construction camps. These and other incidents are believed to have been responsible for the death of at least three Los Angeles water-system guards.

Fruit and vegetable growers in Santa Clara Valley had made all the commotion they could. When protests went unheeded they tried an injunction. They didn't get far in the courts; sentiment of judges was weighted by concern that Los Angeles should have water in reserve.

William Mulholland, chief of the Los Angeles Bureau of Water and Power, was no amateur. He had spent more than forty years with the system and was universally regarded as an exceptionally competent engineer.

A design was approved, and after extensive litigation the site was acquired. St. Francis Dam was completed in May, 1926, at a cost of more than $1,300,000.

The dam towered 175 feet above the streambed over which it was erected. An additional thirty feet of concrete went into the foundation. At the base the massive structure was 175 feet thick, tapering to a thickness of sixteen feet at the top. Compared with it, a section of the Great Wall of China would seem puny and fragile.

Best engineering standards of the day were used. There was no reason that the dam should not last indefinitely.

No reason from the viewpoint of engineers who designed and executed the massive rigid structure, that is.

In the grim postmortem that followed failure of the huge dam that was not yet two years old, expert opinion concluded that the basic weakness was geological. Strong as it was, for practical purposes St. Francis Dam had feet of putty.

It was built across San Francisquito Canyon about fifteen miles above Saugus. This location afforded an ideal site for impounding vast quantities of water that could be held in storage until needed, then moved quickly to the city by aqueduct.

One side of the valley site was made up chiefly of mica schist.

Unlike granite such rock is not even approximately homogenous. Instead it is a mixture whose ingredients tend to form numerous thin layers that do not adhere strongly to one another.

Mica schist had never given any trouble; there was no reason to expect it would now. But across the canyon the other wing of the dam was anchored to a valley wall of quite different type. Superficially strong, the conglomerate that formed it was a type of poorly bonded rock that contained many pieces of gravel and other detritus.

Because the conglomerate was notoriously unreliable, engineers compensated by erecting a superstrong and heavy dam. With a base 175 feet thick it was felt that the structure didn't need a great deal of support at the sides.

That reasoning may have been valid. But it failed to give adequate weight to an all-important factor. With mica schist at one side of the canyon and conglomerate at the other there was no rigid body of bedrock beneath the dam.

Far worse, in the aftermath of the tragedy was the discovery —too late—that near the center of the canyon, conglomerate and schist were separated by a wide zone of shearing. Within this geological fault powerful earth forces had reduced rocks to powder and had then recompressed them.

It was this mass of material that lay directly beneath the dam.

A lengthy trial followed failure of the structure. In a tense courtroom drama a deputy district attorney asked to make what he called "a basic demonstration." With permission granted, he displayed in one hand a glass of water and in the other a chunk of what seemed to be ordinary rock. Workmen testified that the rock came from the area on which St. Francis Dam had been built.

Dropped into water, the heavy chunk sank to the bottom. While jurors watched, it began to dissolve. Sharp edges disappeared and it took on the appearance of muddy clay. Continuing to explain the composition of the stuff the district attorney placed his hand over the top of the glass and shook it rapidly. Then he stretched out his hand with the prize exhibit of the trial.

"Ladies and gentlemen," he said, "your eyes have already

shown you that this 'solid rock' has quickly become nothing more substantial than a ball of mud."

At the site of the disaster, maintenance men had recognized the possiblity of trouble as early as the morning of March 12, 1928. At Powerhouse #2, located more than a mile below the dam, Dan Mathews found that muddy water was slowly trickling past his post of duty. There had been heavy rains upstream. But the water he saw couldn't possibly be coming over the dam or through the sluice gates. Instead it seemed to be seeping around or under the vast concrete barrier.

William Mulholland, vigorous and forceful at seventy-one, came in person to check the situation when informed of what was happening. He reached the dam about midday, inspected visually and then probed the ground with a shovel at several spots.

"It's a leak, all right," he announced. "Things look bad. But it is our responsibility to see that water is here in case it is needed by the citizens of Los Angeles. We have had too much water in the last few days, but you know we just have to take water as the Good Lord sends it to us."

There was no possible way to stop the seepage, Mulholland concluded. It was not a desirable situation, but it appeared to pose no threat to the 137,000 cubic yards of cement deftly engineered to curve inward and upward in order to impound water from hundreds of square miles of land that drained into upper reaches of the canyon.

There was no general alarm. Even a declaration of a state of potential emergency would do nothing except create confusion, authorities concluded. Hence nothing at all was done to evacuate any of the estimated 20,000 persons whose homes were spread through the valley below the dam.

The official verdict was: "Things do not look good, but the situation will continue to be under control."

About twelve hours after that conclusion was reached, one side of St. Francis Dam gave way. Engineers never did decide positively which side it was, for minutes later the other side buckled too.

Most persons would have considered the big central section to be particularly vulnerable because of the weight behind it.

101

Strangely, this portion of the dam emerged from the catastrophe with little damage.

As one side and then the other broke loose from walls of the canyon, enormous chunks of concrete resting only upon slimy mud were shot forward as though from gigantic guns. Propelled by twelve billion gallons of water surging downward toward the sea, huge fragments of the dam were swept half a mile, three-quarters of a mile, and in one spectacular case slightly more than a mile down the valley.

Roaring water estimated to be eighty feet deep when the wave began rolled forward with such force that everything—literally everything—in a twelve-mile path was swept away.

Because of the hour, traffic was light on California Highway 126, paralleling the Santa Clara River. That was a godsend. So was the fact that the river itself was low. Had it been overflowing from rains like those that had fallen upstream, devastation would have been much worse.

No one ever knew precisely how many cars, most of them carrying two or three persons, were swept away. Some were dug out of mud twenty miles from the highway. A few that washed out to sea were discovered by divers many months afterward. From the list of missing persons, it was estimated that about fifty cars and one hundred to one hundred twenty-five persons died when water roared over the highway.

Near the dam itself more than eighty men were sleeping in a construction camp. Water hit so suddenly that no man had time even to open a tent flap. Logically, every man there should have perished. Most did. But five workmen on cots were picked up by the crest of the wave and lifted to safety almost as though they were surfers on skis.

More than 600 homes were destroyed; more than 700 persons died. No exact list of fatalities was ever established.

The city of Los Angeles conceded responsibility and in less than a week completed arrangements to begin paying claims. Most survivors received death benefits ranging from $7,000 to $10,000 for each relative killed. Farmers got about $3,000 per acre for prime groves that were destroyed and up to $500 an acre for uncultivated land without trees.

Before the last claim was settled, the city had paid out an

estimated $30,000,000 in damages. That was about twenty-five times the cost of St. Francis Dam.

In the aftermath of the tragedy it was generally agreed that future dam construction should involve participation by geologists as well as by engineers. Since 1928 this principle has generally been followed in public construction—though it has been conspicuously violated by some coal mine operators and other big land owners.

Used as a case history in many engineering courses, the story of St. Francis Dam hammers home the point that safety of a structure is not determined by its body alone. Unless its feet are able to support it, sooner or later it will give way.

*April 21, 1930*
*Columbus, Ohio*

# 17 Inferno at Ohio State Prison

Responsibility for safety of imprisoned men and women is one of the first principles of American penal codes. Members of the Ohio state legislature, along with Governor Myers Y. Cooper and officials of the state's prison system, were conscious of that responsibility.

But they did little to relieve conditions when overcrowding of the state penitentiary at Columbus was repeatedly denounced by inmates, visitors, and newspaper reporters. Failure to live up to responsibility concerning safety measures converted the prison into a deathtrap in which 317 men died.

Facilities at Columbus were designed for 1500 inmates. By 1929, the prison was packed with more than 4,000 men. New contingents arrived every week.

"The Columbus prison has become one of the nation's biggest," pointed out the annual handbook of the National Society of Penal Information. "Overcrowding has added to hazards that exist wherever persons are kept behind locked doors. The Ohio institution is too crowded to provide acceptable standards for housing prisoners."

That 1929 indictment gave the entire state of Ohio a black eye. As a result of national publicity, work on a new cellblock was accelerated. When finished it would accommodate enough men to give a bit of relief in older sections of the prison. Besides, it would be a showplace that would dull the edge of criticism.

According to practically all witnesses who testified in formal hearings after the tragedy, fire started in scaffolding of the new cellblock. Some 800 men marching from supper to their cells in the west block of the penitentiary saw the flames just before sundown.

There were questions and objections from the group of marching men, but prisoners were told to "Shut up, and move faster!" Guards who had worked there for years were proud of the fact that the prison was fireproof. Caution indicated that all inmates should be secured before attention was diverted to the blaze.

Guards went through usual security measures, accelerated a trifle and saw that every man was behind bars. Just as the last bolts clanged into position, a burst of wind carried flaming embers from the "harmless" construction area to the roof of the prison. That roof was built of wood covered with tarpaper. Cement and steel formed the floors and walls, but no one had thought of the roof.

Once a small blaze was started there, the flammable material burned rapidly. Within minutes the "fireproof" structure was an inferno. Flames roared along oil-soaked rafters, then leaped downward to engulf the mattresses and bedding of top-floor bunks.

About this time firemen received the first alarm—from a box outside the penitentiary. A passerby had seen smoke and ran to call for help. Inside the prison the telephone was busy with calls to officials of state and federal military units. Consequently the first contingent of armed men arrived at about the same time the first hook-and-ladder truck screeched to a halt outside the locked gates.

Inside the west block all doors had been locked two or three minutes before the 6:00 p.m. hour prescribed by regulations. Billowing smoke sent inmates into frenzy. One prisoner seized a chisel and tried to force open his cell door. It was just beginning to yield when a guard shot him dead.

Minutes later sections of the roof began to collapse. Each cell became a separate furnace. Thickening smoke made it impossible to see and drove dozens of gasping men to the floor.

In the aftermath of the tragedy a special board of inquiry appointed by the governor heard a great deal of damning testimony.

Guard Thomas Watkinson, members of the board of inquiry solemnly concluded, had refused to hand over to other guards the keys of cellblocks in which men were suffocating. When his comrades took keys from Watkinson by force, it was too late; many doors were already so hot that locks were warped and keys no longer functioned.

Except in the west block guards managed to get practically everyone out. With their bayonets held at the ready, troops prodded prisoners into a compound where fire could not reach them.

A few inmates went berserk and tried to cut fire hoses. Others started secondary fires in the hope that these diversions would provide an opportunity to make a break. Only one prisoner got away during the pandemonium. He exchanged his stripes for a civilian suit and slipped into the crowd of onlookers.

Partly because Warden Thomas had relegated much authority to his 71-year-old chief deputy, J. C. Woodward, many routine precautions had been taken casually. No fire drill had been held among prisoners within the memory of any guard. Even guards and deputies had received no instructions concerning what to do in case of fire.

Emphasis was on security measures designed to keep inmates from escaping or causing trouble. On this point the prison was incredibly efficient.

Having had no instructions, drills, or experience in dealing with fire many guards proved resourceful and brave. So did many prisoners.

With flames licking toward him one inmate who had seized a sledge hammer refused to run. He hit blow after blow, knocking locks from cell doors and saving the lives of an estimated 136 trapped men.

Outside the gates of the prison ranks of friends and relatives of inmates were swelled by the merely curious. When gates opened to admit firemen, the mob tried to storm inside too.

Guards armed with rifles and tear gas turned their attention from prisoners to civilian rioters. By the time they beat the mob back so that firemen could enter in an orderly fashion, the worst of the carnage was over.

Prisoner-volunteers assisted guards in bringing out the bodies. Many had choked to death. Some were burned beyond recognition. Laid on the fresh green grass of the prison yard, victims whose clothing had been burned away could not even be recognized as men who had been wearing stripes.

More than two hundred inmates who were overcome by smoke and who suffered severe burns were put into guarded wards of hospitals. All of them eventually recovered. Meanwhile, bodies that had been temporarily stored in a big cattle shed were given "decent burial."

Throughout the nation newspapers condemned the lax administration that permitted all the ingredients of catastrophe to accumulate. In Ohio editors were particularly forthright. Responsibility for the holocaust, said the Columbus *Evening Dispatch*, rested squarely upon the state of Ohio. In Cleveland, the *Plain Dealer* asserted that "the cries of men behind steel bars who were held in a vise for creeping flames to destroy" were pleas that never again would any state permit prisoners to be housed in a deathtrap.

Thomas Watkinson, the guard who had refused to unlock burning cellblocks, was suspended by the prison warden. The official board of inquiry placed responsibility upon the prison administration but meted out no punishments.

Aroused legislators, not merely in Ohio but in many other states, took action to relieve some of the more flagrant abuses and dangers. Most authorities on state and local levels added fire drills to the routine of prison life, and stricter codes for construction of prisons were enacted.

In spite of these reforms, the nation's worst prison fire remains a grim reminder that every step aimed at adding to security measures also adds to potential dangers of men behind locked doors.

August 14, 1933
Northwestern Oregon

## 18  The Great Tillamook Forest Burn

Until shortly after 1:00 P.M. on the afternoon of August 14, 1933, the forest lookout station near the top of Saddle Mountain looked down on one of the world's finest stands of virgin timber. Douglas firs more than four hundred years old, taller than ten-story buildings and measuring five to twelve feet in girth, stretched as far as the eye could see in every direction.

Suddenly a wisp of smoke was sighted. It seemed to be coming from Gales Creek Canyon, where several logging crews had big operations in progress. Experience indicated that these veteran woodsmen would be able to get the blaze under control very quickly. Still, crews of professional fire fighters were dispatched as a precaution. No one could remember when the forest had been so dry; fire would spread much more quickly than usual.

By the time smoke was sighted, the blaze had already fanned out many yards in every direction from the point of ignition. Garbled and conflicting testimony by woodsmen made it difficult for investigators to establish the cause of the blaze. At first it was believed to be the work of incendiaries. One official panel accepted testimony that a sudden thunderstorm produced a single mighty lightning flash that struck a tinder-dry forest giant and set it afire. But the weight of evidence supports the informal reports of loggers who were working in the canyon. Because humidity was low and heat was intense, most crews were pulled off the job early in the day. One wildcat outfit ignored hazards that were multiplied by a brisk northwest wind and tried to get out a few extra logs. Pulled by steam through the underbrush, the heavy trunk of an enormous fir hit the powder-dry stump of a tree felled years earlier and the impact produced fire by friction.

As logging accidents go, it was a minor one. There were no injuries to members of the crew, and the tree with which they were working continued to snake its way toward the donkey engine that provided power for the operation. Fire by friction is not unusual in the big woods, and normally yields to ten minutes of conventional fire fighting.

This was not a normal situation. There had been no rain in days. Heat of the sun was so great that much underbrush was near the kindling point, ready to erupt upon receiving a relatively small amount of additional energy. The bark of big trees was so dry that once they caught fire, they smoldered for hours after being doused with water—then burst into flames again.

More than one hundred men, called from half a dozen nearby fire stations, hurried into Gales Creek Canyon to help loggers who were already doing their best. From the outset it was a losing battle. Fire spread more rapidly than men and machinery could make fire lines. To make things worse, heat was so intense and wind was so brisk that at intervals the blaze "crowned," jumping from a blazing treetop across a cleared space into the tops of the forest giants fifty, sixty, even seventy yards away.

Truckloads of CCC workers raced to the stricken area, joined ranks of fire fighters, and worked all night without a break. In Portland, sixty miles to the east, city dwellers scanned headlines of the Sunday morning paper and clucked their dismay at the idea of having a canyon full of fine trees set afire by some clumsy logger or by "a pyromaniac out on a binge." By noon that Sunday the mood of the whole region had changed. Emergency messages went to nearby cities. Volunteers piled into trucks in Portland, Salem, and Vancouver and waved cheerful good-byes to their families as they left for what they expected to be "a few hours of hard work." Experts from the Pacific Northwest Forest Experiment Station and the U. S. Forest Service arrived and took command. All night truckloads of volunteers poured into the vast Tillamook region.

"It all proved useless," said Lynn Cronemiller in retrospect. "In my years as Oregon's state forester I never saw anything that even approached this burn. The most we ever succeeded in doing was to hold the line temporarily; at times we were positively overwhelmed. There was just one life lost—a CCC boy from Indiana who was killed by a falling tree. But lumber destroyed by the blaze was roughly equivalent to all the boards and planks turned out by all the sawmills in the U. S. during the entire year 1932."

Cronemiller said that "Most of the really costly damage was done to Douglas firs. There were thousands of them that took root about the time Columbus discovered the New World." The tree takes its name from Scottish botanist David Douglas (1798-1834) who explored much of the Pacific northwest on expeditions for Britain's Royal Horticultural Society. Douglas "discovered" the great tree in 1825 and was so awed by it that early descriptions were not believed by Europeans who read them. E. D. Buell of the Oregon-American Lumber Company estimated that "about 80% of the timber killed in the Tillamook Burn was Douglas fir; western hemlock accounted for 15%; the rest was equally divided between red cedar and miscellaneous species."

Roaring along a fifteen-mile front, smoke billowed so high that fine ashes began to fall in Portland. A mushroom of smoke, hundreds of times as large as typical thunderstorms, hung at an altitude of about 8,500 feet.

Both singly and in droves, deer and other animals tried to flee from the flames. In their fear of the fire they lost all fear of humans, often brushing against fire fighters in panic-stricken flight. Even the swiftest of forest creatures seldom made it to safety. Tens of thousands ran into canyons that seemed safe but soon burst into flames and cremated the animals who had taken refuge there.

Never fully contained, the great fire subsided at sporadic intervals during ten days of continued drought. During this period, an estimated 40,000 acres of timber burned.

On the eleventh day weary fire fighters saw a drama unequaled on the American continent. A sudden shift of wind thwarted efforts of more than 3,000 men. Flames leaped across two hundred feet of clear ground into new stands of virgin timber. During the next twenty hours the fire roared over 270,000 acres until fog drifted in from the coast and hampered the demon's progress sufficiently to enable fire fighters to overcome it.

Atmosphereic pollution caused by the blaze was beyond calculation. Sinclair A. Wilson of the Pacific Northwest Forest Experiment Station pointed out that "along the coast, ashes, partly burned branches, and debris from the fire piled up more than twelve inches deep." More particulate matter was ejected into the atmosphere during those twelve days than is usually put there in a year.

Timber that was killed would have yielded almost two billion board feet of fine lumber. In the case of forest giants whose gaunt trunks remained standing after all branches burned away, six-inch bark was reduced to charcoal that dropped off at the slightest touch.

Some timber remained sound beneath the blackened surfaces. Salvage operations were slow and costly, but began immediately and were still proceeding when the Japanese bombed Pearl Harbor. Spurred by the war effort, loggers took hundreds of millions of board feet of lumber from the Tillamook area during 1942-43.

In uncontrolled fury, irreparable destruction of wildlife and pollution of the air plus ratio of economic loss to human death, Tillamook reigns supreme as the king of all United States forest fires. Economic loss to Oregon was conservatively estimated at more than $200,000,000.

Still, the long-range effect of the catastrophe was positive. It served to trigger eventual changes in public opinion and in conservation methods. Programs of education aimed at prevention of forest fires were given new impetus. Regulations governing

111

activities of logging crews were made more stringent in Oregon and most other timber-producing states. In all of our national parks additional watchtowers were constructed and heavy-duty fire-fighting equipment was added. So in the decades since the great Tillamook Burn trees and animals saved from possible destruction by fire greatly exceed even the number killed in the twelve-day inferno that was launched by a single careless action.

September 8, 1934
*Off the New Jersey Coast*

## 19 Final Hours of the *Morro Castle*

From cruise-happy landlubbers to gnarled seamen, most persons acquainted with the Ward liner *Morro Castle* agreed that she could not burn. Her mechanical fire-fighting equipment was the last word.

Even in the event of a blaze it would have seemed ridiculous to fear loss of life. She was seldom more than a few hours from land and was almost always in the middle of a busy shipping lane. There was an ample supply of life preservers—hardly necessary, it seemed, since boats and rafts offered space for 470 persons above her usual quota of passengers and crew. As though that were not enough, she carried two sets of radio equipment and could call for help in any emergency.

When the luxury liner burned just seven miles off the coast of New Jersey, owners and operators called the disaster "an act of God." But the public and the courts rejected this verdict and laid the blame on blundering officers and crew members.

There were plenty of safety devices aboard the *Morro Castle*, but all of them proved useless when the human equation broke

113

down. It all started—though passengers didn't know it—when Captain Wilmotte decided to take a bath. Jovial, plump, and fifty-five, he was commodore of the Ward Line fleet.

In all his thirty-one years at sea Wilmotte had commanded no vessel comparable to the *Morro Castle*. He liked to think of her as a floating hotel with all the usual luxuries, plus a fine sea breeze. From dance hall to dining rooms she offered the best. Tonight the captain's dinner would make a man glad he had a good appetite.

Captain Wilmotte never ate that dinner. He settled into a hot tub to relax, then soon began groaning for help. "Acute indigestion from a bath with a full stomach," grunted the ship's doctor after a hasty examination. When he filled out the death certificate he simply wrote: "Heart attack."

Unaware of impending doom passengers reacted to the news by protesting cancellation of planned festivities. While they consulted stewards about small private parties, First Officer William Warms hurried to the bridge and took command. It was a proud moment for him, an opportunity he had been anticipating for years.

Warms was still on duty when sparks were seen seven hours later. John Kempf, a Long Island fireman who had booked passage for the cruise, later testified that he smelled smoke as early as midnight. His evidence was supported by stewardess Harriet Brown, who declared that the linen room was "intolerably hot" at that hour. But the first official recognition of danger came at 2:55 A.M. on September 8, 1934. Acting Second Officer Hackney saw smoke and sparks coming from the stokehole. He rang the engine room to inquire about fire; learning nothing, he pulled an alarm.

Meanwhile a few stewards had been fighting flames for at least a quarter of an hour. A woman passenger had wandered into the writing room and had found the roof blazing. Called to put it out the watchman advised her not to make a commotion that would disturb sleepers. Stewards had some difficulty finding hoses, and none remembered the location of the nearest water connection. By the time an alert reached the bridge the flames had eaten through thin wooden partitions into a ventilator shaft.

Like most vessels built for the tropics, the *Morro Castle* was riddled with air channels, portholes, and ventilators. Fire spread through these natural flues. Then it leaped into chimney-like elevator shafts. Outside, a twenty-mile wind was whistling against the liner—which was plowing straight into it at 19.2 knots. Every open porthole fed forced air into the combustion area.

By the time officers were aroused, it was too late to confine the blaze by closing steel fire doors. Spreading up and down elevator shafts and stairways flames soon had the effect of dividing the vessel in half. Insulation burned off electrical wiring and created short circuits. This threw much of the ship into darkness and crippled the telephone system. Unable to sound a general alarm officers sent stewards through corridors banging on pots and pans to awaken passengers.

Captain Warms rejected suggestions that drastic action be taken. After all, they were only half an hour from shore—headed for Ambrose Channel to pick up a pilot. By the time they got there, fire fighters would surely have things under control.

So the *Morro Castle* continued on course, speed unchecked. Those few passengers who jumped from lower decks in early panic were pulverized by the ship's big screws or left behind to drown.

Warms knew nothing of conditions in the stern. As minutes passed, however, it became clear that matters were getting worse. He decided to alter his course so that wind would sweep flames clear of the deck rather than toward staterooms. So he sent signals to the engine room ordering the port propeller to be stopped, with full speed on the starboard propeller.

Just as the ship neared the end of its quarterturn, remaining electric circuits failed. Foghorn and whistle went dead. Electric pumps stopped. Gyropilot and steering gear ceased to function.

Dark and out of control, the death ship continued in its arc. Engine crews shut down boilers to prevent an explosion, but by the time propellers stopped at 3:31, the vessel had made a complete circle. Wind-whipped flames fanned out in every direction.

From the beginning of the confusion, passengers had found it difficult to reach the boat deck. More than 200 of the 316 aboard gathered in the stern of the vessel. Some failed to bring life preservers from staterooms, so there were not enough to go around.

There were few signs of hysteria. Men, women, and children stared at the advancing flames. A young priest climbed a ladder and offered final absolution. A half-dressed businessman defiantly led a chorus in singing "Hail, Hail, the Gang's All Here." A fur-clad matron opened her coat to cover the shoulders of a stenographer who was shivering in her negligee. Peering into a fire-lighted mirror, one passenger gaily repaired her makeup.

Few members of the crew remained with stranded passengers. Most of them used service passages to reach the boat deck. There balsa life rafts, light and easily launched, offered a quick way off the doomed liner. Junior electrician Joseph Penner broke out one raft and managed to get it into the water. But eleven others designed to carry seventeen persons each burned before they could be launched.

Engines had hardly stopped throbbing before seamen lowered boat #10 without waiting for orders from officers. Seven members of the crew plus three women passengers took off—in a boat with space for forty-eight.

Chief engineer Eben S. Abbott had been roused from sleep so suddenly that he left his false teeth beside his bunk. Without once visiting the engine room he gave telephone orders that the second and third engineers should stay at their posts. Abbott himself left the bridge to go on an inspection tour.

His hasty survey came to an abrupt end when he jumped into the #3 lifeboat. Tackle jammed, so Abbott left Seaman Joseph Spilgis in charge and took command of the #1 boat. Less than half-filled—with twenty-nine members of the crew and two passengers—it pulled away from the blazing ship. Abbott ripped braid from his coat in a desperate attempt to surrender responsibility according to later testimony. "I was in a dazed, dizzy condition," he said to a board of inquiry.

Tackle cleared, boat #3 was launched with sixteen members of the crew aboard. Boat #11 took off with an equal number of seamen plus a single passenger. Boat #5 jammed halfway to the water so was abandoned for #9. Loaded with seven men—10 percent of capacity—the craft headed for the Jersey shore. In desperation a sailor later slid down a cable and hacked #5 free; four men crawled aboard, broke out oars, and rowed away.

Boat #10 reached shore through heavy surf at about 6:00 A.M. Five others beached between 7:00 and 9:00. With total capacity of 408, these boats brought eighty-five persons to safety; most were members of the crew. A night watchman later swore that he led fifty passengers to the promenade deck only to have two nearly empty lifeboats refuse to wait for them.

Naval experts who investigated the hulk of the death ship found six boats burned in the davits. There was evidence of an attempt to lower #7. Nothing indicated such efforts in relation to lifeboats #2, #4, #6, #8, or #12. William F. Price, a passenger, testified that, "There was no member of the crew around these boats; we stayed there for an hour and a half hoping someone would come."

Long before the first boat was launched, a quarrel broke out between Warms and his radiomen. Charles Maki, third operator, was on duty when the fire was discovered. He routed out his superiors, who raced to the radio shack fifty feet aft of the bridge. Rogers, chief operator, sent George Alagna for orders. He ran back to say that he found Captain Warms in a daze, muttering over and over: "Am I dreaming, or is it true?"

Scuttling back and forth at Rogers' insistence Alagna finally told his chief, "They're a bunch of madmen up there on the bridge."

Desperate, Rogers took matters in his own hands and at 3:15 sent out a CQ without orders. This cleared the air but did not appeal for help. Captain Warms, afraid that his employers would have to pay salvage fees, refused to authorize an SOS. At 3:17 he gave permission to repeat the "standby" signal.

Most radio equipment was already out of commission due to power failure. Now the batteries in the emergency receiver were beginning to explode from heat. In a matter of minutes the emergency transmitter was likely to go out.

Finally the acting captain yielded to Alagna's pleas. Scurrying back to the radio shack he gestured to his chief. Using the emergency transmitter, at 3:24 Rogers began tapping his key: "Di-di-di da-da-da di-di-di. MORRO CASTLE AFIRE TWEN-

TY MILES SOUTH OF SCOTLAND LIGHT, CANNOT HOLD OUT MUCH LONGER."

Twenty-eight minutes after a state of emergency was recognized, the first—and only—SOS went out. Nearly a quarter of an hour earlier the freighter S. S. *Andrea Luckenbach* had radioed Coast Guardsmen at Tuckerton, New Jersey, to ask if there was a big ship blazing off Sea Girt. Guardsmen had received no distress signal and could not see flames through seven miles of rain.

The Coast Guard noted Rogers' SOS at 3:24. A quick check showed the *Morro Castle* to be only four years old, flagship of the Ward Line. With a beam of 70.9 feet and length of 508 feet she had capacity for more than four hundred passengers.

It would be a major rescue operation. Coast Guard boats were called from all nearby stations: Cape May, Shark River, Barnegat, Sandy Hook, Spermacetti Cove, Deal, Long Branch, and Spring Lake. They began swarming out within minutes, but few had any equipment other than dories manned by four oarsmen. It would be a major battle to get through the surf.

Three nearby deep-sea vessels caught Rogers' single desperate appeal. Seven miles west the freighter *Andrea S. Luckenbach* had already caught glimpses of fire. Twenty miles north the liners *Monarch of Bermuda* and *City of Savannah* turned toward the burning ship. Their radio messages went unanswered; by this time even emergency equipment of the *Morro Castle* was out.

With half of her lifeboats launched and the rest abandoned, the stricken vessel drifted out of control. Her starboard anchor, dropped in desperation, merely dragged. Without stopping the liner it served to swing her bow into the wind and throw flames nearer the mass of refugees huddled in the stern.

Few acted hastily. Lillian Wallace had vaulted through flames to reach the deck, but she pulled on a life belt and sat quietly for two hours before jumping overboard. Una Cullen, a stenographer, had been staging a small party. Still wearing high heels and a trailing velvet gown she moved about chatting and joking.

Lighted only by ghastly flames the choppy sea was hardly more inviting than the doomed vessel. Veteran travelers declared there was a strong smell of land; perhaps they could hold out until morning.

Gouveneur Phelps saw the end coming about 5:00 A.M. Rising winds, pushing intermittent banks of rolling fog, threatened to sweep the decks with fire at any instant. He jumped, swam to a rope hanging from the stern, and clung there until picked up by a rescue boat.

Men, women, and children jumped singly and in small groups until only about one hundred remained on deck. Arthur Sheridan, eight, was afraid to jump. His mother pushed him overboard—and saw him drown before she hit the water. Charles and Selma Filtzer, married just one week, jumped hand-in-hand. They found a floating corpse and buoyed themselves on it for four hours. Then a huge wave took the bridegroom under.

Gray dawn was breaking over gunmetal surf when the first rescue boat arrived. Manned by five Coast Guardsmen, the 26-foot craft was soon filled. At 7:30 the *Monarch of Bermuda* launched four small boats that picked up seventy-one survivors. Seamen from the *Andrea S. Luckenbach* rescued twenty-one, and the *City of Savannah* picked up sixty-five.

Three fishing smacks, on the way to their morning catch, sighted the fire and turned aside. John Bogan, owner of the *Paramount*, pulled sixty-seven into his little vessel. "It was the most horrible sight I ever saw. The water was full of dead," he said.

Incredibly, William Warms and fourteen men still clung aboard the gutted ship when met by rescue tugs. Taken aboard the cutter *Tampa*, Warms insisted that he would not be responsible for tow charges. Alagna testified that they were met by a Ward Line attorney when they reached shore.

"Now, boys," he cautioned them, "this terrible thing which has occurred is entirely an act of God. The U. S. Attorney will come aboard and want testimony, and I advise you to ignore him completely. If you are not careful, he will garble everything and you will just make trouble for yourselves and everyone else. You'll be taken care of. . . ."

Confronted by an official investigation, line officials blandly announced their defense. Loss of the *Morro Castle*, they said,

119

was "due solely to fire and/or inevitable accident and/or Act of God and/or acts of public enemies."

Finding little official tendency to place the blame directly on Almighty God, attorneys for the line whooped up a communist scare. Under the Harter Act arson on shipboard was defined as an act of God involving no civil liability on the part of owners. Claiming a red plot, Ward Line officials disclaimed responsibility for loss of 134 lives. Action was filed by which the line's financial responsibility would be limited to three assets: "passage money, $13,358.71; freight charges, $2,489.43; present value of the beached wreck, $600.00."

Dickerson N. Hoover, Inspector general of the Steamship Division of the U. S. Department of Commerce, led an official inquiry. Analysis of Captain Wilmotte's ashes (his body having been cremated on the death ship) showed no trace of poison. There was nothing to support charges of a communist plot.

Plenty of unsavory evidence turned up, however. Only seven men were on duty when the fire broke out; two of the three watchmen were too busy serving passengers to make their rounds. There never had been a fire drill for passengers—Captain Wilmotte had not wished to alarm them. No members of the crew knew the location of heavy fire doors that could have confined the blaze to a single section. Flammable enamel and brass polish were stored aboard. Joseph Spilgis, in charge of starboard lifeboats, testified that they would have sprung leaks if scraped before the last painting.

Angelo Vlaco, shipping master who hired the crew, couldn't read or write. He hadn't been to sea in thirty-five years, and when a man was hired he was asked few questions except whether he'd work for rock-bottom wages.

In spite of the fact that seamen made up ninety-two of the first ninety-eight to abandon ship, Ward Line rested its defense on the plea that the vessel and not the men had failed in an emergency. Jurors listened to ten weeks of testimony, then retired for ten hours of deliberation.

Their decision was without precedent in American maritime history: deck officers, the operating line, and a shore official were convicted and sentenced. Imposing a $10,000 fine on Ward

Line, Judge Murray Hulbert said: "The penalty imposed by the Statute is insufficient."

Appealed to a higher court, jail sentences for Warms and Abbott were set aside. Blame for the disaster was placed on Captain Wilmotte. Had he maintained proper discipline and organization, ruled the United States Circuit Court of Appeals, his staff would have functioned without him.

Meanwhile the owners of the liner collected insurance amounting to more than $250,000 above book value of the *Morro Castle*—and offered to settle death claims at $150 per head.

Relatives and survivors refused these terms. Two years after the disaster, in September, 1936, the steamship company allocated $890,000 for settlement of liability claims. Most litigants accepted settlement from this total.

They did not stop at partial financial redress. Organized as "the *Morro Castle* Safety at Sea Association," they pressed for national reforms. For five years a subcommittee of Congress had sat on legislation to make the United States accept the International Convention for Safety of Life at Sea, already ratified by most major shipping nations.

Now the *Morro Castle* disaster brought the act out of committee and to the floor of Congress where it won quick ratification. Official and private investigations brought sweeping reforms in the entire U. S. merchant marine. Sprinkler systems were made mandatory throughout passenger ships. Radio laws were modernized, and the Federal Marine Inspection Service was enlarged.

Because public sentiment refused to equate blundering incompetence with an act of God, all Americans travel in safer vessels manned by better crews.

*January-February, 1937*
*Ohio-Mississippi Valley*

# 20 The Ohio-Mississippi Valley Flood of 1937

"Disaster #2,128."

That's the way the Ohio-Mississippi Valley Flood of 1937 is labeled in records of the American Red Cross. Some standard reference works do not devote so much as one line to the flood.

Yet the official report of relief operations of the American Red Cross points out that, "the Ohio-Mississippi Valley Flood of 1937 was, next to the World War, the worst disaster in the history of the nation. In a sense, there were concentrated in one calamity as many problems as might be expected in thirty-two average years of minor disaster activity."

Reference books may neglect it, but no one who lived through the flood can ever forget it. Thirty-five years afterward Mrs. Lois Glindmyer of Rotterdam Junction, N.Y., recalled it even more vividly than her experiences as a nurse in World War II.

"I was about fifteen at the time. We lived in a suburb of Jeffersonville, Indiana, known as Midway. There were nine in our family and I recall being taken from our home with nothing except what we could carry in our hands.

"We were first housed in a nearby school. When the water kept rising we were taken by boat to a bus that transported us to the fairgrounds in Indianapolis. As we went through the station after reaching Indianapolis, I can remember people lined up to watch us and I can still hear a voice saying: 'Don't touch them; they may be diseased!'"

Strangely it was the nation's worst peacetime disaster before 1972 that elevated the American Red Cross to new prominence and gave it a permanent place among influential institutions.

"Flood relief was one of the earliest major activities," according to Dr. Albert G. Hahn, former director of Protestant Deaconess Hospital in Evansville, Indiana. "In 1884 Red Cross workers helped flood victims here. Miss Clara Barton, director and founder of the organization, came to the banks of the Ohio to check on the progress of relief work."

Chartered and reasonably well financed, the organization went through a period of steady growth. Then governmental agencies spawned by the New Deal assumed more and more responsibility for activities related to those of the Red Cross.

Almost eclipsed by the federal bureaucracy the private charitable-humanitarian organization lost ground.

According to Foster R. Dulles, disasters during the spring of 1936 helped revive public interest in the Red Cross, "but they were actually to prove only a curtain-raiser for the even greater catastrophe of the next year. The Ohio-Mississippi flood established new records all along the line. Once again the Red Cross was able to demonstrate that it could do a job that Government agencies were not immediately prepared to undertake when disaster struck suddenly and unexpectedly."

January brought moisture-laden storm clouds to the midwest. That is not unusual. This region often experiences heavy rain during this season. What made the 1937 clouds unique was their incalculable bulk and their stubborn refusal to move eastward toward the sea.

During that one month, say U. S. Weather Bureau records, water dumped into the Ohio River drainage basin amounted to "at least 156,000,000,000 tons of rain."

In recorded history no other rainfall upon the North American continent has been so big. During a period of about ten days enough water was dumped from the skies to cover the state of Pennsylvania to a depth of forty-four inches.

By January 22, persons living near rivers knew they were in for trouble. Many of them moved out with the hope of returning by the weekend. Hour after hour the big, heavy drops pelted down. By January 24, more than one million persons were designating the day by the label, "Black Sunday."

As long as roads and rails were above water, trains and trucks were used to evacuate flooded regions. But before midnight on Sunday all land transportation and communication had halted over a vast area. Army, Navy, Coast Guard, Marine, and Public Health Service units were mobilized. So were the C.C.C. and the W.P.A., along with hundreds of state and local agencies.

It proved impossible for any governmental unit to handle the crisis. Coordination between them was lacking, and a state of emergency was rapidly approaching.

From West Virginia to Louisiana, 196 counties in twelve states were flooded. More than 12,700 square miles of land were actually submerged. Final tabulations indicated that 12,860 homes and other buildings were destroyed, while another 60,792 were damaged.

Refugee centers and tent cities sprang up throughout the flooded area. Wherever large permanent buildings such as those on the grounds of the Indiana State Fair were available, they were used as shelters. At the call of Admiral Grayson, national chairman of the Red Cross, thousands of nurses poured into stricken areas.

Three of them left Newburgh, Indiana, for Owensboro, Kentucky, at 3:30 P.M. on January 25. "The river was reaching its crest and the thermometer was dropping rapidly," they later reported. "We made progress at the rate of two miles an hour.

"It took us twelve hours to cross the Ohio. In Owensboro the situation was distressing. On landing, we immediately rushed to a refugee center. This center, established by the local chapter of the Red Cross, became an emergency hospital. For the first seventy-two hours we were there we stayed on our feet without a break, treating and inoculating victims of the flood."

124

With variations that story could be repeated hundreds of times. For before the angry waters subsided the Red Cross established 1,757 refugee centers and tent cities that cared for more than 698,000 persons.

In Evansville, grimly labeled "an American Venice," the local Red Cross chairman was thrown from a capsizing boat. He clung to a lamppost until another vessel came along.

At the height of the emergency one of the most critical needs was for boats. Many were turned over to the Red Cross by the Navy Coast Guard, the Tennessee Valley Authority, and U. S. Army Corps of Engineers. Hundreds of others were borrowed or chartered from private owners. Several manufacturing plants shut down their usual operations and made flat-bottom boats. As a result of all this coordinated activity, during a period of just five days the Red Cross assembled a flotilla of more than 7,000 boats.

Serum, food, and clothing were sent to stricken areas. Doctors and nurses left their ordinary duties and offered their services.

Even animals were not forgotten. Along with refugee camps for humans made homeless by the rising waters, the Red Cross set up stockades for livestock and deer plus shelters for many of the tens of thousands of homeless dogs and cats. Many emergency kennels were built adjacent to refugee camps. Some 250 lives were lost, and property damage was eventually estimated at $300,000,000. Every major city along the Ohio River and most on the lower Mississippi were affected. The timetable for Evansville, Indiana, was typical:

January 21—Forecast of 47.7 feet river stage was made.

January 22—Record flood expected; weather bureau warned: "Prepare for at least 51 feet."

January 23—River reached 48.4 feet; Red Cross substations and contagious disease hospital were set up.

January 24—Martial law was declared. Weatherman Mclin S. Collom died in his office from strain of working around the clock.

January 25—Colonel Louis L. Roberts, National Guard commander, issued military rules limiting use of gasoline and coal. About 300 blocks of the city were under water.

January 26—At 1:00 P.M. the Ohio reached 52.24 feet. Business was suspended, waterworks shut down, electric power cut off in many areas.

January 25—Red Cross established drinking water stations. Tank cars sent to bring supply to city. Water was strictly rationed. More than 400 blocks now flooded.

January 28—Red Cross announced plans for rehabilitation program. Last bridge to west side of city closed.

January 29—Red Cross administered typhoid shots to last of 35,000 persons who may have been exposed.

January 30—Crest of 53.74 feet was reached; over 500 blocks of city were under water. Red Cross officials asserted that they were "confident that funds will be found to meet critical needs of all flood victims."

That's the way it went up and down the mighty Ohio River during that fateful last week of January. "We got help from everywhere," reported Chairman Grayson. "Inmates of a Louisiana prison sent $63. Children contributed pennies. A former Red Cross nurse who had no money sent her uniform as a gift."

Corporations, individuals, and governmental units put their response was everywhere evident, public support soared. Total the nation's biggest coordinated effort short of war. The original goal for flood relief was small; chapter quotas were increased only as it became clearly evident that larger amounts would be required. When the goal reached $10,000,000, the national headquarters stopped assigning quotas.

As magnitude of the flood became apparent and Red Cross response was everywhere evident, public support soared. Total gifts amounted to $25,565,680—more than eight times the annual income of the Red Cross in preceding years. This fund broke world records for a peacetime disaster appeal. It still ranks as the biggest of all private United States relief efforts.

Assessing the impact of the flood, in 1938 Admiral Grayson said: "This national disaster buried once and for all the idea that government should substitute public for voluntary financing of disaster relief." Boosted into new esteem by having shown its capacity to cope with a disaster too big for any of many competing tax-supported agencies, the American Red Cross became *the* troubleshooting agency of the nation.

March 18, 1937
New London, Texas

# 21 Explosion of the New London School

"The roof just lifted up. Then the walls fell out and the roof fell in."

That terse description by William C. Shaw, superintendent of the Consolidated School at New London, Texas, indicates the brevity—but not the heartache—of a tragedy that stemmed from undue concern for saving a small amount of money.

The Consolidated School was located in the heart of one of the world's great oil fields. A person could walk from room to room and look out of the windows to see nothing but oil rigs in every direction. On a clear day, using the school as an observation point, at least 10,000 derricks could be spotted with the naked eye. Eleven of them stood on the school's grounds.

Oil meant money. Money meant liberal expenditures. Royalties from oil wells within the school grounds yielded most of the million dollars with which an old wooden schoolhouse was razed in order to be succeeded by one of the most elaborate rural educational facilities in the United States. There were laboratories, home economics kitchens, lecture rooms, and play-

127

grounds of the finest quality. Multimillion-dollar expenditures for education became commonplace four decades later; in the 1930's it was rare for a school district—urban or rural—to erect facilities without regard for cost.

Pupils came from an area thirty miles square. Still there were only 1,500 of them in handsome modern buildings whose initial cost had exceeded $1,000,000.

It was the crude oil of East Texas that brought in the money. But civic leaders in the booming town were not yet accustomed to ceaseless flow of easy cash. In the aftermath of an explosion that left at least 297 students and faculty members dead, administrators were accused of "being free with their dollars and stingy with their pennies."

This charge grew out of an economy move that was made in January, 1937. Until then, Union Gas Co. had sold the New London School Board a natural gas mixed with a pungent odorant. Because such commercial gas was abundant and cheap, fuel bills for the school amounted to only $250 to $350 per month. Not much money, to be sure, but enough to show up in financial statements. Why pay for commercial gas when a substitute could be had for nothing?

Reasoning in this fashion school authorities decided to discontinue purchasing processed gas. They authorized the superintendent to bring in workmen who would tap into a pipeline carrying away waste gas from a big plant operated by the Parade Oil Co.

Waste gas had plenty of fuel value. It was doing nobody any good so long as it was being thrown away. Why not give the school board a little elbow room by eliminating the gas bill entirely?

Officials of Parade Oil Co. later testified that they had not authorized the tapping of their waste gas line. But they knew about it and had not objected.

Burning of waste gas was a common practice in New London and in other towns located close to oil fields. Everyone knew the stuff was a mixture of several components and that the heating capacity (and ignition point) varied from day to day and even from hour to hour. Still it caused few problems—and it cost nothing.

Dozens of business establishments and homes in New London had been heated with it for months before members of the school board decided it was too good to be wasted. Since classrooms were heated by individual radiators, the educational complex used a lot of gas.

At 3:05 P.M. on Thursday, March 18, 1937, the main building of the Consolidated School exploded. The mighty first blast was followed by a series of smaller ones that were hardly noticed in the tumult. Oil field workers heard the roar for miles around, hastily shut off their pumps, and raced to the scene of the disaster.

"Thank God!" one parent exclaimed as he reached the scene; the primary grades had been dismissed before the blast.

But an estimated 690 high school students who would have been out of the building in another ten minutes were waiting to hear the bell that signaled dismissal. More than forty teachers were still in classrooms.

Within an hour after the explosion the school yard was crowded with bodies of the victims. Early reports by the Associated Press estimated the casualty toll at about 455 children "crumpled under steel and concrete or squeezed bloodless by the blast." Revised downward several times, the official figure finally stopped at 297 students and teachers. That meant the oil field blast was the biggest American disaster, in terms of lives lost, since the burning of the *General Slocum* in 1904.

More than half of the 437 students and teachers who got out alive had to be hospitalized for injuries. Some were left with lifelong handicaps. A few had escapes that their loved ones could only term "miraculous." Crawling into the dusty ruins with two other men, Don Nelson found a heavy bookcase tipped against the wall. Pulled upright it was revealed to be a sturdy shelter under which ten pale children had been preserved.

Some of the dead were killed so quickly that they still had smiles on their faces when they were found. Others were mutilated beyond recognition. When the number of unidentified bodies began to approach four dozen, authorities sent to Dallas for fingerprints. On a field trip, most of the New London students had visited the Texas Centennial Exposition a year earlier and had been fingerprinted there.

A hasty search through the debris turned up a half-empty case of dynamite. Sorrow and bewilderment of the townspeople turned to rage. Who would be so low as to dynamite a school building just minutes before it was scheduled to be emptied?

Even before police began to search for possible culprits, fresh evidence emerged. Experts who examined the ruins shook their heads in dismay and concurred that "indisputable evidence" pointed to an explosion caused by the fuel used to heat the buildings.

Notoriously unstable and commonly called "raw" or "wet" by oil field workers, waste gas was widely recognized to be far more dangerous than the commerical or "dry" variety from which impurities had been removed. Some persons who deliberately took the risk involved in use of wet gas adapted their equipment to handle it. Members of the New London School Board had agreed that it would be a waste of money to adapt radiators designed for use of dry gas.

Testimony concerning dynamite was given during the long-drawn official inquiry that followed the disaster, but this evidence was brushed aside as irrelevant. According to testimony of school superintendent Shaw, whose own son of seventeen died in the blast, the decision to save money by tapping into the waste line of Parade Oil Co. was implemented as soon as it was authorized by the board. It would have been costly to call in trained workmen to undertake the dangerous job. So the school janitor had been instructed to install a connection that would pipe waste gas through the basement to the school's radiators. University of Texas expert E. P. Schoch testified that if just one of the school's main lines was accidentally left flowing for half a day, "the saturation point" would be reached, creating conditions for a potential explosion.

Official verdicts came later. According to findings of the board of inquiry the blast actually was caused by an accumulation of the volatile wet gas. Presumably it was ignited by a spark. Courts declined to name the source of that spark. Perhaps it came from a light switch. Perhaps it resulted from a buildup of static electricity.

On the day of the tragedy such matters were mentioned only in passing. Everyone who could move was too busy shuttling

130

bodies to inquire into details of the events that led up to the tragedy. Bodies were placed in trucks, then trucks moved in a steady line to improvised morgues. First-aid stations quickly overflowed not only in New London but also in Tyler, Overton, Kilgore, and Henderson.

All during the night survivors tried to identify bodies laid out in New London's Methodist Church and in private homes. In nearby Pleasant Hill Cemetery shifts of workers were busy digging 300 graves. A consignment of 200 coffins arrived from Dallas; officials wired for more.

Governor James V. Allred was informed of the catastrophe by telegraph. At first he was inclined to consider reports "greatly exaggerated." As more details trickled into his Austin office, he concluded that even if the initial estimates were drastically reduced, the tragedy would surpass any in the history of public education in the United States.

Reaction to the tragedy was immediate and decisive. Even before the board of inquiry released its official findings, lawmakers in oil-producing states moved to avert a repetition of the New London disaster. As a result oil companies throughout the nation are now required by law to burn their unprocessed "wet" gas at site. Any person or institution now using this dangerous stuff for heating purposes is doing so illegally and in secret.

Newsmen who rushed to the Texas community in the aftermath of the blast concurred that the most ironic product of a tragedy that needn't have occurred was right on top of the wreckage. Blown out of the ruined building that housed most classrooms was a section of blackboard. Only hours before the blast some student in an elementary grade had scrawled on the blackboard:

Oil and natural gas are East Texas' greatest natural gifts. Without them, this school would not be here and none of us would be learning our lessons.

December 7, 1946
Atlanta, Georgia

# 22 Flaming Terror at the Winecoff Hotel

Built in 1913 by Atlanta's W. Frank Winecoff, the hotel that bore his name was considered by architects to be "the latest thing in high-rise construction." Walls and floors of the hotel were of steel-reinforced concrete plus terra cotta, faced with brick and marble. Dividing walls between rooms were of hollow tile. Since none of the major components of the structure would burn, city ordinances placed it in the fire-resistant category. Privately both operators and Atlanta officials regarded it as absolutely fireproof. Consequently it was not equipped with fire escapes—they seemed superfluous and "would have detracted from the simple beauty of the building."

Fire broke out at about 3:00 A.M. on Saturday, December 7, 1946. Because of its construction the building itself suffered little damage except from smoke and water. Inspected only a few weeks before the blaze, the Winecoff had met all safety regulations. But occupants of the building remained vulnerable to side effects of fire. Few, if any, burned to death, but smoke inhalation plus desperate leaps from upper stories cost lives

132

of at least 119 persons. One of them was F. W. Winecoff, who continued to reside there after he leased the building to a holding company.

Tall and narrow, the Winecoff went straight up. There were fifteen stories and about two hundred rooms. Most rooms were at levels above the reach of aerial ladders. Lacking fire escapes to which they could flee, occupants for the most part braved smoke and terror until they could hold out no longer. Some jumped for big nets held by firemen many stories below; others simply plunged.

Bill Mobley, 35-year-old chief night bellboy, was among the first to smell smoke. Walking with the building engineer between the fourth and fifth floors on a routine checkup Mobley insisted that a guest room nearby was on fire. A hasty inspection revealed that the telltale odor was coming from one of the two stairways in the tall, narrow building.

Mobley later said that he yanked the stairway door open and was hit in the face by a blast of hot air. "I was already scared," he said. "I looked quickly and found that flames seemed to be coming up the stairs from the fourth floor. That stairway made a kind of natural chimney with a powerful draft. Flames never slowed up. They moved up the face of the wall, which had just been given a coat of fresh paint, almost like a baseball moves off the bat."

Mr. and Mrs. F. A. Herring woke up at 3:30 in their room on the third floor. Herring, auditor for the hotel, said he believed that at least 275 guests were registered. Many were delegates to a state youth conference.

"Before my wife and I could put on our clothes we saw bodies begin to hurtle past our windows," Herring said. "We knew we couldn't make it to the ground, so we covered our heads with blankets and turned on the fans. We kept our door shut, and didn't move until firemen came through a window and rescued us."

Comer L. Rowan, night manager of the hotel, reported that he learned of the catastrophe about 3:30. An elevator operator ran to Rowan's room and shouted, "The hotel is burning like a dry haystack!"

Rowan hurried to the hotel switchboard and began making

133

emergency calls to guests. "I couldn't say much to anyone," he said. "Time was short. But I urged those to whom I talked to be sure that their doors were closed, to prevent drafts that might spread the flames."

Only a fraction of the persons trapped in the burning building received Rowan's calls; of these only a few heeded his advice. Many had left transoms open so that they might get a bit of fresh air. Combined with open windows, these ducts caused fire to race along hallways after enveloping elevator shafts and stairways.

Patrolman N. W. Smith of the Atlanta Police Department was first to arrive at the scene. Captain L. J. Carroll joined him within two minutes. "By the time the captain ran into the lobby all elevators were out of commission," Smith testified. "We fought our way upstairs, kicking on doors and breaking into some rooms in order to arouse as many guests as we could. When we reached the seventh floor we saw we couldn't go on, and turned back."

Reporter George Goodwin said that, "By the time I answered the call a few minutes after four o'clock, it looked as though the whole Atlanta Fire Department was on hand. Aerial ladders lifted spider-like into the smoke. All swarmed with firemen and survivors from the lower floors. From windows of upper floors scores screamed and begged for help. Already, a number had jumped."

Mrs. Alice Ann Gilbert, eighteen, of Portland, Oregon, was among the handful rescued from the eleventh floor. Married just three days earlier she repeatedly moaned, "Where is my sweetheart?" as she was rushed to a hospital by ambulance. Eventually located, Gilbert was found to be uncomfortable from smoke inhalation but otherwise all right.

Scores were less fortunate.

Mrs. A. R. Minnix of Columbus, Georgia, was rescued from her room on the fifth floor. She became hysterical when she realized that her fifteen-year-old son was trapped in his room on the eleventh floor. "We didn't want to separate," she explained, "but they couldn't give us rooms on the same floor."

Brought to the sidewalk by city firemen, Mrs. Frank Smith of Valdosta, Georgia, revived from unconsciousness just long enough to sob: "My ten-year-old daughter! She was standing on the ledge!"

Survivors reported that the first victim to plunge to death was a girl of about fourteen. For a time she was seen dangling from an upper floor window by a sheet. Eventually she turned loose and plunged to the sidewalk.

Arthur Cheatham, state director of the veterans' service, saw two girls who were more fortunate. "They jumped from the tenth floor," he said, "and firemen who saw them coming managed to get nets under them. Miraculously, both were saved. Just then a tall man swung down from a window on a rope, trying to reach the top of a ladder. A firemen started up to get him—then someone jumped or fell from above. There was a direct hit; almost as if in slow motion all three men plunged toward the ground."

On the sixth floor where Nelson Thatch had his quarters, the chief room clerk of the hotel tried to persuade a woman not to jump from a window. "She hesitated an instant," Thatch reported. "Then she turned away from me and whirled from her perch. She hit cobblestones in the alley behind the hotel and died on impact; I never knew her name."

James Little, of Elizabethton, Tennessee, saw his friend Frank Jones of Friendship, Tennessee, plunge in panic from the eighth floor. "I tried to keep him from jumping, but couldn't stop him," Little said. "If he had only waited another five minutes he would have been rescued, too."

Reporter Chick Hosch saw four women leap to their deaths. "I got there about forty-five minutes after the alarm went out," he said. "From my position I saw fifteen or twenty persons jump. None walked away, but several of them hit nets and had their falls broken enough to save their lives."

Of the 119 who died, at least 25 jumped from upper floors. Only a few persons suffered serious burns. Far the greatest toll was taken by smoke inhalation and asphyxiation from lack of oxygen. In addition to deaths there were at least 168 injuries, of which more than half were termed serious.

Of the 49 delegates to the state youth conference registered at the hotel, at least thirty-two of the teen-agers died. Initial estimates of "about 275 guests" were later revised upward to "more than 300." Newspaper reports said that of these, only seventeen got out of the hotel without injury.

Damage to the building was superficial. It needed no structural repairs, only redecorating. Long before dawn on the fatal morning it was clear that the death toll would greatly exceed that of America's worst hotel fire on record. When Newhall House burned in Milwaukee in 1883, seventy-one persons died; no other U. S. hotel disaster had claimed so many lives.

World interest in the holocaust in a building officially classified as fire-resistant was so great that from 7:00 A.M. Saturday until late afternoon, telephone lines were busy most of the time. First to call from overseas was Reg Cudlipp, city editor of *News of the World*, published in London.

Georgia's Solicitor General E. E. Andrews launched an official probe only a few hours after the blaze was extinguished. He came to the conclusion that it was started by a cigarette carelessly tossed into a mattress stored in a third-floor hallway.

Atlanta Fire Chief C. C. Styron was quoted as being in general agreement with that finding. A spokesman for operators declared that "insurance coverage is more than adequate." He proved to be right—so far as the building was concerned. But millions of dollars in damage suits forced the hotel into receivership.

In the aftermath of the tragedy Chief Styron pointed out that, "It needn't have happened. A sprinkler system or even a fire detection system might have prevented the whole thing."

Officials of the National Fire Prevention Association successfully pressed for abandonment of the term "fireproof" in codes describing structures used by persons. "It cannot be too strongly stressed," an early official bulletin pointed out, "that no building plus contents can ever be completely fireproof. Regardless of construction methods, any building in which substantial numbers of persons congregate on upper floors needs fire-escape routes other than elevators and stairways."

Atlanta made sweeping changes in her fire laws and building code; dozens of other cities did the same. Partly as a result of these reforms, United States hotels have subsequently experienced hundreds of fires without breaking the ghastly record set the morning the little "fireproof" Winecoff burned.

*July 2-19, 1951*
*Kansas and Missouri*

## 23 The Kansas-Missouri Flood of 1951

White adventurers who pushed into the valleys of the Missouri, Mississippi, and Arkansas rivers while the vast region was still dominated by native Americans found it subject to devastating floods. The area now known as Kansas, they learned, is particularly vulnerable.

Engineers later discovered the reason. Much of the region known as "the breadbasket of the nation" slopes gently from west to east. This downward slope averages only seven feet per mile, so it cannot be seen with the eye. In time of high water it is great enough to be devastating. Danger from floods is magnified by big areas where winds have caused great erosion, for eroded land does not easily absorb or hold water.

Kansas has seen many floods. One of the worst of modern times hit in 1903, taking at least thirty-eight lives. In the aftermath of that disaster Kansas City and many other communities increased the height of their dikes and built new ones. Army engineers warned that these measures were stopgap at best; dikes alone could never control major floods in the plains, they warned.

137

Congress and the legislatures of affected states discussed a long-range and costly program of flood control, but compromised far short of the elaborate system of upstream spillways and reservoirs that engineers recommended.

During a period of forty-eight years there were several floods, but none was of catastrophic nature. Veteran Kansas weather experts warned of potential trouble as early as May, 1951; it was the wettest May in the state's weather history. June did not bring welcome relief—but more burdened clouds. When they dropped their billion-gallon loads on the already water-soaked state, they made the month the wettest June in modern times.

With the flood not yet at its crest, turbulent waters swept into Kansas City on July 13. Hundreds of thousands of acres of land had poured two months' accumulation of rain into the swollen Missouri River, famous locally as "the Big Muddy."

Communication systems had been altered radically since Ohio-Mississippi Valley flood of 1937. This time practically all persons in affected areas had plenty of time to get out before their lives were endangered. A few chose to stay, but 200,000 fled from their homes. Deaths were rare; drowning, accidents, and sickness linked with high water caused only forty-one fatalities. But property damage mounted day after day, eventually reaching a peak "somewhere above or below one billion dollars."

In Kansas City, where some of the hardest blows were delivered, three major industrial districts were under water by July 14. Fire started in an oil storage tank area of two square blocks. Gasoline, diesel oil, and naphtha filled tank after tank; though firemen fought around the clock for four days, more than a dozen tanks exploded to spew 850,000 gallons of blazing fuel on top of racing flood waters.

Mayor William E. Kemp had already issued emergency orders requiring all nonessential businesses to close. A transportation crisis was clearly in the offing, and the water supply of the metropolis, already greatly reduced by flooding of the Turkey Creek pumping station, was threatened.

Major General Lewis Pick, Chief of U. S. Army Corps of Engineers, tabulated reports of damage already done and projected effects that might be expected as the crest moved slowly southward. "We are facing a national emergency brought on by our own failure to spend money for control," he said. "Now we are going to have to dig deep into our individual and national pocketbooks in order to help victims of this flood."

With a metropolitan population of 900,000, Kansas City involved more persons than all other affected cities and towns combined. In Lawrence (population 20,000) flooding was limited to the northern district of the city. Topeka, with 100,000 population, saw more than one-fifth of her citizens evacuated. Wichita, warned to prepare for the worst, was saved by a freak of nature. So much driftwood accumulated in swollen rivers that the speed of water was reduced enough to spare the city from severe flooding.

Along most of the watershed of the Missouri River and in many areas where its swollen waters caused the Mississippi to flood, bridges were washed out. Airports were submerged. Telephone and telegraph lines were down. From Junction City, Kansas, close to the mouth of the river that Plains Indians knew as the Kaw, all the way to Kansas City nearly every town and city was closed to railway traffic. Flooded tracks left occasional islands of safety where trains stopped and their crews waited for the waters to subside.

Not far from Wichita the famous transcontinental train El Capitan was stranded with 337 passengers aboard for more than fifty-five hours. Rancher Bill Brandt of Burns, Kansas, used U. S. Highway 508 as a landing strip and made fifteen trips to bring supplies and water to the train, evacuating ill passengers as he left.

With turbulent muddy water stretching to the horizon the shortage of drinking water became one of the most urgent problems in stricken areas. A fire truck from Newton, Kansas, brought 1,000 gallons to passengers marooned in the El Capitan train at Cedar Point. Pure water was strictly rationed in regions as far distant as Kansas City and suburban St. Louis.

Square mile after square mile of farmland covered with grain nearly ready for the harvest went under water. Before the carnage was over, an estimated 850,000 acres of wheat and corn were flooded.

Power failures plus flooding brought a crisis in the industrial area where Armour, Swift, Wilson, and Cudahy packing plants

139

were located. Army engineers began on July 15 the task of removing as much of the twenty-five million pounds of meat as possible. Using boats, meat was taken to big refrigerated trucks in "Operation Porkchop"—still notable as the biggest meat-lift in recorded history.

Livestock trapped in the Kansas City stockyards were in no great danger but began to suffer discomfort as they stood hour after hour with water first covering their hooves, then rising to their knees, to their bellies, and finally to their necks. More than 10,000 head were evacuated to higher ground.

By July 18, federal aid was on the way. By unanimous vote, the House of Representatives had passed a bill providing for $25,000,000 in relief money. Hastily pushed through the Senate, it was signed by President Harry S. Truman only a few hours after he returned from a personal tour of inspection of stricken areas in Kansas, Oklahoma, and his home state of Missouri.

Officials of the American Red Cross mobilized chapters in more than two dozen counties and helped with evacuation of threatened communities. Red Cross president E. Roland Harriman made a nationwide appeal for $5,000,000 in special funds for relief and rehabilitation of flood victims. Nearly 10 percent of the national quota was assigned to Manhattan, the Bronx, and Queens, where 30,000 volunteers assumed the task of solicitation and collection of gifts.

Robert Edson, Red Cross disaster relief director of the sixteen-state Midwest Area, stressed that the funds sought could do nothing more than "alleviate the most pressing needs." He described the loss of homes in Kansas City as almost unbelievable, said, "Except for the water and silt you would think tornadoes had gone through the area."

Supplies of powdered milk, eggs, and cheese were made available from the Department of Agriculture. Portable water purifying units were provided by the Public Health Service and flown in from distant points. Officials of the Labor Department reported that three of its seven offices in the stricken region were flooded, but that records had been saved. As a result, they said, unemployment insurance could be paid to covered workers made idle by the raging waters. Emergency field examiners were sent by the Reconstruction Finance Corporation to administer a disaster fund of $35,000,000 designated toward helping to put homes in preflood condition.

Measured against the impact of economic losses ranging close to one billion dollars, all relief measures combined could only provide temporary and token assistance. It was up to the farmers and householders and merchants and manufacturers of the region to recoup their own losses as best they could.

In the end, however, the costly flood brought changes that had been advocated for many years. As early as 1944, the Army Corps of Engineers and the Bureau of Reclamation had prepared a detailed master plan for flood control in the 530,000-square-mile great plains region that produces more wheat than any other section of the world.

Legislators had examined plans and pronounced them worthy but "too expensive." Now it was clear that hundreds of millions spent on reservoirs and spillways, as well as bigger and better dikes and levees, would mean vast economic benefits in the event of future floods. Both federal and state governments acted relatively promptly; municipal governments did what they could too.

Most experts concur in the verdict that potentially catastrophic floods will continue to visit the breadbasket of the nation. Probabilities are that such floods will come "once or twice every century." There is no way to predict when they will come, no way completely to tame their fury.

Yet the likelihood of anything approaching the 1951 disaster in the foreseeable future is remote. Flood control work already completed in the drainage basin of the Missouri River would keep most of the region high and dry in the event of a repetition of the wettest May and wettest June in the history of the Weather Bureau.

# Bibliography

Many bibliographies concentrate chiefly upon sources used in preparing the books to which they are attached. Here the emphasis is broader. Information concerning the disasters described in this book has come chiefly from newspapers and periodicals. Some, though now recognized to have played vital roles in influencing the development of North America, are so obscure that they are not even listed in standard works that give brief information about major catastrophes. Hence the volumes listed here are chiefly for the information of readers who wish to pursue particular interests, or wish to extend their knowledge about disasters in general.

Valuable lists appear in these volumes of information published annually:

*Family Almanac* (compiled by the research department of the *New York Times*)—major disasters and catastrophes in the Christian era are listed in chronological order.

*Information Please Almanac*—approximately one dozen categories in which various kinds of major disasters are briefly described.

*World Almanac*—with diasters grouped into categories, editors attempt to give accurate information in capsule form.

*Reader's Digest Almanac*—again grouped by categories, most disasters of modern times are reported in one line each.

[Note that though all these standard volumes of information seek high standards of accuracy, they do not offer identical lists of disasters, and in numerous cases their reports vary somewhat.]

Annual volumes of information are helpful when newspapers and periodicals are not available. Numerous publishers of encyclopedias issue yearbooks in which catastrophic events occupy significant space.

Especially helpful is the *Annual Register* of world events published since 1758.

Some of the more useful and interesting modern books dealing with various kinds of disasters are:

Andrews, Ralph W. *Historic Fires of the West.* New York: Bonanza Books, 1966.
Armstrong, Warren. *Last Voyage.* New York: John Day, 1956.
Baldwin, Hanson W. *Sea Fights and Shipwrecks.* New York: Hanover House, 1955.
Barnaby, Kenneth C. *Some Ship Disasters and Their Causes.* Cranbury, N.J.: A. S. Barnes, 1970.
Bennett, Geoffrey. *By Human Error.* London: Seeley Service, 1961.
Bixby, William. *Havoc: The Story of Natural Disasters.* New York: McKay, 1961.
Boyer, Dwight. *True Tales of the Great Lakes.* New York: Dodd, Mead, 1971.
Clevely, Hugh. *Famous Fires.* New York: John Day, 1958.
Corbett, Edmund V. *Great True Stories of Tragedy and Disaster.* New York: Arco, 1961.
Downey, F. D. *Disaster Fighters.* New York: Putnam's, 1938.
Gallagher, Thomas. *Fire at Sea.* New York: Rinehart, 1959.
Haywood, Charles Fry. *General Alarm.* New York: Dodd, Mead, 1967.
Hewitt, Ronald. *From Earthquake, Fire and Flood.* New York: Scribner's, 1957.
Hoehling, A. A. *Great Ship Disasters.* New York: Cowles, 1971.
Kartman, Ben, and Brown, Leonard. *Disaster!* New York: Pellegrini & Cudahy, 1948.
Lockhart, John G. *Peril of the Sea.* New York: Stokes, n.d.
Morris, John V. *Fires and Firefighters.* Boston: Little, Brown, 1955.
Porges, Irwin. *Many Brave Hearts.* New York: Chilton, 1962.
Snow, Edward Rowe. *The Fury of the Seas.* New York: Dodd, Mead, 1964.
Snow, Edward Rowe. *New England Sea Tragedies.* New York: Dodd, Mead, 1960.
Snow, Edward Rowe. *The Vengeful Sea.* New York: Dodd, Mead, 1956.
Sutton, Ann, and Sutton, Myron. *Nature on the Rampage.* Philadelphia: Lippincott, 1962.